COOKING WITH
CRAFT BEER

MORE THAN 100 RECIPES MADE WITH CRAFT BEER

Publications International, Ltd.

Louis Weber, CEO
Publications International, Ltd.
7373 North Cicero Avenue
Lincolnwood, IL 60712

Pictured on the front cover: Beer-Fa-Lo Wings with Blue Cheese Dip *(page 38),* Cheddar-Beer Burgers with Bacon *(page 96)* and Spicy Smoked Beef Ribs *(page 156).*

Pictured on the back cover *(clockwise from top left)*: Best Beef Brisket Sandwich Ever *(page 96),* Fish and Chips *(page 158)* and Soft Beer Pretzels *(page 68).*

ISBN: 978-1-68022-089-6

Library of Congress Control Number: 2015934783

Manufactured in China.

8 7 6 5 4 3 2 1

Microwave Cooking: Microwave ovens vary in wattage. Use the cooking times as guidelines and check for doneness before adding more time.

Publications International, Ltd.

TABLE OF CONTENTS

WHAT'S ALL THE BREW-HAHA?

Beer, by definition, is an alcoholic beverage produced through fermentation. It is traditionally made from water and malted grains, such as barley, and flavored with hops. The grains used during production release sugar, which feeds the yeast added during production. This yeast, in turn, fuels the slow fermentation process. The placement of the yeast during fermentation is a key factor in determining the outcome of the beer. Bottom-fermented beers are made with yeast fermenting at the bottom of the barrel, whereas top-fermented beers hold the yeast at the top of the barrel. While there are some alternate methods of using yeast, most beers fall into one of these two classifications. Bottom-fermented beers, or lagers, are typically light in color with high carbonation. Top-fermented beers, or ales, produce a wider variety of beers—from pale ales to stouts—ranging in everything from flavor to color.

In order to differentiate between beers and have a better understanding of the different types available, it is crucial to identify a few factors used to describe beer. The first and most easily identifiable quality is **appearance**, which includes the color, clarity and head of a beer. Once a beer is opened or poured, the **aroma** becomes evident. From there, **flavor** can also be identified. The flavor is often broken down as the balance between the bitterness of the hops, sweetness of the malt and tanginess of the yeast. Beyond the overall taste of a beer, flavor can be broken into smaller elements such as the taste and amount of malt used in production, as well as the flavor of the yeast used and the resulting bitterness. **Mouthfeel**, which includes both the thickness and carbonation of a beer, ranges greatly in different types of beers. And the **strength** of a beer, or the alcohol content, also helps to categorize different beers.

> The ways to use beer in cooking run the gamut from braising meats and simmering stews to baking desserts.

Beer is one of the most popular beverages in the world, but it's good for more than just imbibing. Beer can serve as an ideal cooking liquid, adding depth and flavor to a plethora of dishes. The ways to use beer in cooking run the gamut from braising meats and simmering stews to baking desserts. In order to identify the best beer to use for cooking, it is crucial to first understand the characteristics of each beer. Although many factors will affect the outcome of a dish, appearance and flavor are the two most helpful indicators. A light, crisp beer will add subtle flavor without significantly changing the color of a dish, whereas a darker beer will impart a slightly heavier flavor and should be used for hearty dishes such as stews and long braises. Below is a breakdown of a few of the most common varieties of beer, listed from light to dark.

BLONDE ALE
One of the palest beers available, these ales tend to very clear. They have a crisp, dry flavor with a slight bitterness.

PILSNER
This clean and simple lager is one of the most popular beer varieties. It is pale and fragrant. They have a slight to somewhat strong bitterness, depending on the variety and amount of hops used during production.

WHEAT BEER
While wheat styles and flavors differ, these beers are typically light in flavor. Some feature yeast as the most dominant flavor, while others take on a slightly spicier note. They are made with a mixture of barley and wheat grains and very little (if any) hops, and they tend to be slightly cloudy in appearance.

PALE ALE
Both English and U.S. pale ales are copper colored as a result of the gently roasted barley used in production. While both have robust flavors, English pale ales tend to have a strong malt flavor and U.S. pale ales are spicier.

INDIA PALE ALE
This hoppier version of the English pale ale is made in a similar fashion but with more hops. The result is a stronger taste that is slightly bitter.

AMBER/RED ALE
Named for its color, these balanced ales feature notes of toasted malts and range in hoppiness. Some also have hints of fruitiness or caramel. (Amber lagers are also available.)

IRISH RED ALE
This beer features a slightly sweet flavor that is reminiscent of tea. It has a rounded and balanced flavor of toasted malts and a dry finish.

BROWN ALE
Ranging in color from dark amber to brown, the higher level of malts used in production make these beers more earthy and less bitter. While some can be sweet and slightly hoppy, others have a malt-heavy flavor.

BOCK
Stronger than the typical lager, bocks use more malt in production and have a more prevalent malt flavor. This creates a rich flavor with hints of bitterness from the hops.

PORTER
A dark, nearly opaque ale made with roasted malts or roasted barley. The flavors of the roasted grains are evident, but the taste is still mild with hints of chocolate.

STOUT
This extremely dark, thick beer is made with black, unmalted barley. It has a heavily roasted flavor that regularly features notes of coffee or molasses, which often covers up the flavor of the hops. Stout is also known for its thick, creamy head.

BEER BITES

MUSSELS WITH AIOLI AND CROUTONS
MAKES 4 SERVINGS

1 loaf (1 pound) French bread, cut into ¼-inch slices

AIOLI

½ cup mayonnaise

2 cloves garlic, minced

2 tablespoons olive oil

2 teaspoons lemon juice

½ teaspoon Dijon mustard

⅛ teaspoon ground red pepper

MUSSELS

1 tablespoon olive oil

1 shallot, chopped

1 bottle (12 ounces) craft-brewed lager or other light-colored beer

¾ cup water

4 pounds mussels, scrubbed and debearded

1. For croutons, preheat oven to 450°F. Toast bread on baking sheet 15 minutes or until golden brown on both sides, turning once.

2. Meanwhile, prepare aioli. Combine mayonnaise, garlic, oil, lemon juice, mustard and ground red pepper in small bowl; mix well. Cover and refrigerate.

3. Heat oil in large saucepan over medium heat. Add shallot; cook and stir 1 minute or until translucent. Add lager and water. Increase heat to high; bring to a boil. Carefully add mussels. Cover and cook 3 to 5 minutes or until mussels open. Remove from heat and cool slightly. Discard any unopened mussels.

4. Spread each crouton with 1 teaspoon aioli. Serve mussels and broth in bowls with croutons.

BACON AND CHEESE RAREBIT

MAKES 6 SERVINGS

1½ tablespoons butter

½ cup craft-brewed lager or other light-colored beer

2 teaspoons Dijon mustard

2 teaspoons Worcestershire sauce

⅛ teaspoon ground red pepper

2 cups (8 ounces) shredded American cheese

1½ cups (6 ounces) shredded sharp Cheddar cheese

1 small loaf (8 ounces) egg bread or challah, cut into 6 (1-inch-thick) slices

12 large slices tomato

12 slices bacon, crisp-cooked

Minced fresh parsley (optional)

1. Preheat broiler. Line baking sheet with foil.

2. Melt butter in double boiler set over simmering water. Stir in beer, mustard, Worcestershire sauce and ground red pepper; cook until heated through, stirring occasionally. Gradually add cheeses, stirring constantly until melted. Remove from heat; cover and keep warm.

3. Arrange bread slices on prepared baking sheet; broil until golden brown on both sides, turning once. Top each slice with two tomato slices and two slices of bacon. Spoon about ¼ cup cheese sauce evenly over each. Broil 4 to 5 inches from heat just until cheese sauce begins to brown. Garnish with minced parsley. Serve immediately.

BEER-BATTERED SWEET POTATO FRIES AND ONION RINGS WITH LEMON-THYME AIOLI

MAKES 4 TO 6 SERVINGS

Lemon-Thyme Aioli (recipe follows)
2 sweet potatoes (about 6 ounces each), cut into ¼-inch-thick sticks
2 cups all-purpose flour
1½ cups cornstarch
2 tablespoons paprika
2 teaspoons baking powder
1½ teaspoons salt
¼ teaspoon ground red pepper
2 bottles (12 ounces each) cold craft-brewed lager
Vegetable oil
1 medium onion, cut into ½-inch-thick rounds and separated into rings

1. Prepare Lemon-Thyme Aioli; set aside.

2. Place sweet potato in colander and rinse under cold running water. Blot dry with paper towels; set aside.

3. Combine flour, cornstarch, paprika, baking powder, salt and ground red pepper in large bowl. Slowly whisk in beer until completely smooth.

4. Preheat oven to 200°F. Heat 3 inches of oil in Dutch oven until it reaches 350°F; adjust heat to maintain temperature.

5. Add one third of onion rings to batter, stirring to coat. Shake off excess batter and add to hot oil. Fry in small batches 4 to 5 minutes or until golden brown and crisp, stirring occasionally to prevent sticking. Remove to wire racks or paper towels to drain; keep warm in oven. Repeat with remaining onion rings.

6. Add one fourth of sweet potatoes to batter, stirring to coat. Shake off excess batter and add to hot oil. Fry in small batches 7 to 8 minutes or until golden brown and crisp, stirring occasionally. Remove to wire racks or paper towels to drain; keep warm in oven. Repeat with remaining sweet potatoes. Serve immediately with Lemon-Thyme Aioli for dipping.

LEMON-THYME AIOLI:

Combine ½ cup mayonnaise, 1 tablespoon water, 2 teaspoons lemon juice, 1 teaspoon finely grated lemon peel, ½ teaspoon minced fresh thyme, ¼ teaspoon white pepper and ⅛ teaspoon minced garlic in small bowl. Cover and refrigerate until ready to serve.

MAPLE-MUSTARD PORTER RIBS
MAKES ABOUT 8 SERVINGS (2 RIBS EACH)

1 cup craft-brewed porter

½ cup maple syrup

3 tablespoons Worcestershire sauce

2 tablespoons spicy brown mustard

1 teaspoon salt

¼ teaspoon black pepper

⅛ teaspoon ground red pepper

2 pounds pork baby back ribs, membrane removed from underside, cut in half

1. Combine porter, maple syrup, Worcestershire sauce, mustard, salt, black pepper and ground red pepper in medium saucepan over medium-high heat. Bring to a boil. Reduce heat to low; simmer until reduced to ¾ cup, stirring occasionally. Transfer to large bowl; cool to room temperature.

2. Set oven rack to middle position and preheat oven to 350°F. Line rimmed baking sheet with two layers of foil; spray with nonstick cooking spray.

3. Place ribs in marinade, turning to coat evenly. Arrange ribs, meaty side down, in single layer on prepared baking sheet; brush with remaining marinade. Cover tightly with foil. Bake 50 minutes or until tender.

4. Remove foil and turn ribs meaty side up. Brush ribs with liquid from baking sheet. Heat broiler without moving oven rack; cook until ribs are glazed, brushing ribs every 3 minutes with remaining liquid from baking sheet. Let cool 10 minutes; transfer to cutting board and cut into individual ribs.

WARM CRAB AND BEER DIP
MAKES 8 SERVINGS

12 ounces cream cheese, softened

½ cup finely chopped red bell pepper

½ cup mayonnaise

½ cup craft-brewed pilsner

¼ cup finely chopped onion

¼ cup chopped fresh parsley

1 egg

1 teaspoon hot pepper sauce

¼ teaspoon salt

12 ounces crabmeat*

Pita chips

* Pick out and discard any shell or cartilage from crabmeat.

1. Preheat oven to 375°F. Spray 1-quart baking dish with nonstick cooking spray.

2. Combine cream cheese, bell pepper, mayonnaise, beer, onion, parsley, egg, hot pepper sauce and salt in medium bowl; mix well. Gently fold in crabmeat. Transfer to prepared dish.

3. Bake 35 minutes or until bubbly and browned on top. Let stand 10 minutes. Serve with pita chips.

 ★ **Tip** ★

This dip is also great served with assorted
vegetables, breadsticks, crackers or pretzels.

MINI BEER, BEEF AND POTATO TURNOVERS

MAKES 18 TO 22 TURNOVERS

    Beer Tarragon Mustard (recipe follows)
2 tablespoons olive oil
1½ cups chopped onions
  2 cups chopped mushrooms
½ teaspoon salt
½ teaspoon dried thyme
⅛ teaspoon black pepper
1½ cups chopped cooked steak
1½ cups diced cooked baking potatoes
  2 teaspoons Worcestershire sauce
  1 cup craft-brewed bock
    All-purpose flour
  2 packages (about 15 ounces each) refrigerated pie crusts (4 crusts)
  1 egg
  1 teaspoon water

1. Prepare Beer Tarragon Mustard; set aside.

2. Preheat oven to 350°F. Spray two baking sheets with nonstick cooking spray.

3. Heat oil in large skillet over medium heat. Add onions; cook and stir 5 minutes or until softened. Add mushrooms; cook and stir 5 to 6 minutes. Sprinkle with salt, thyme and pepper. Stir in steak, potatoes and Worcestershire sauce. Pour in beer. Increase heat to high; cook and stir about 5 minutes or until liquid is absorbed. Remove from heat; let cool.

4. Sprinkle cutting board with flour. Unroll pie crusts and cut out circles using 4½-inch cutter. Reroll scraps and cut out additional circles, repeating until all dough is used. Place on prepared cookie sheets.

5. Place 2 tablespoons filling in center of each circle and fold dough over, sealing with fork. Poke with fork to vent. Whisk egg and water in small bowl; brush over turnovers. Bake 25 to 30 minutes or until golden brown. Serve with Beer Tarragon Mustard.

BEER TARRAGON MUSTARD:

Combine ⅓ cup coarse grain mustard, 2 tablespoons deli-style brown mustard, 1 tablespoon chopped fresh tarragon, 1 tablespoon craft-brewed bock and 1 tablespoon honey in small bowl. Cover and refrigerate until ready to serve.

BEER BATTER TEMPURA

MAKES 4 SERVINGS

1½ cups all-purpose flour

1½ cups cold craft-brewed Japanese-style rice lager or pilsner

1 teaspoon salt

Dipping Sauce (recipe follows)

Vegetable oil

½ pound green beans or asparagus tips

1 large sweet potato, peeled and cut into ¼-inch slices

1 medium eggplant, cut into ¼-inch slices

1. Combine flour, beer and salt in medium bowl just until mixed. Batter should be thin and lumpy. *Do not overmix.* Set aside 15 minutes. Meanwhile, prepare Dipping Sauce.

2. Preheat oven to 200°F. Heat 1 inch of oil in large saucepan until it reaches 375°F; adjust heat to maintain temperature.

3. Dip 10 to 12 green beans in batter; add to hot oil. Fry until light golden brown. Remove to wire racks or paper towels to drain; keep warm in oven. Repeat with remaining vegetables, working with one vegetable at a time and being careful not to crowd vegetables. Serve with Dipping Sauce.

DIPPING SAUCE:

Combine ½ cup soy sauce, 2 tablespoons rice wine, 1 tablespoon sugar and ½ teaspoon white vinegar in small saucepan over medium heat. Cook and stir 3 minutes or until sugar dissolves. Add 2 teaspoons minced fresh ginger and 1 clove minced garlic; cook 2 minutes. Add 2 thinly sliced green onions; remove from heat.

SWEET AND SPICY BEER NUTS

MAKES ABOUT 2 CUPS

2 cups pecan halves

2 teaspoons salt

2 teaspoons chili powder

2 teaspoons olive oil

½ teaspoon ground cumin

¼ teaspoon ground red pepper

½ cup sugar

½ cup craft-brewed Irish-style red ale

1. Preheat oven to 350°F. Line baking sheet with foil.

2. Combine pecans, salt, chili powder, oil, cumin and ground red pepper in medium bowl. Spread on prepared baking sheet. Bake 10 minutes or until fragrant. Cool on baking sheet on wire rack.

3. Combine sugar and beer in small saucepan. Heat over medium-high heat until mixture registers 250°F on candy thermometer. Remove from heat; carefully stir in nuts and any loose spices. Spread sugared nuts on prepared baking sheet, separating clusters.

4. Cool completely. Break up any large pieces before serving.

CRISPY CHICKEN NUGGETS WITH PEANUT DIPPING SAUCE

MAKES 6 SERVINGS

DIPPING SAUCE

  ½ cup coconut milk

  ½ cup craft-brewed pilsner

  ½ cup creamy peanut butter

  ⅓ cup packed brown sugar

  3 tablespoons hoisin sauce

  1 tablespoon rice vinegar

NUGGETS

  ¾ cup all-purpose flour

  ¾ teaspoon baking soda

  ¾ teaspoon salt

  ¾ cup craft-brewed pilsner

  Canola oil

  1½ pounds boneless skinless chicken breasts, cut into 1-inch cubes

1. For dipping sauce, whisk coconut milk, ½ cup beer, peanut butter, brown sugar, hoisin sauce and vinegar in medium saucepan. Bring to a simmer over medium heat; cook and stir 3 minutes or until thickened. Transfer to serving bowl.

2. For nuggets, combine flour, baking soda and salt in medium bowl. Whisk in ¾ cup beer until smooth.

3. Heat 2 inches of oil in Dutch oven until it reaches 360°F; adjust heat to maintain temperature. Add 12 chicken pieces to beer mixture, stirring to coat. Shake off excess batter and add to hot oil. Fry 3 minutes or until golden and puffed and chicken is cooked through (165°F). Remove to wire racks or paper towels to drain. Repeat with remaining batter and chicken. Serve immediately with dipping sauce.

PULLED PORK QUESADILLAS
MAKES 8 SERVINGS

1 pound pork tenderloin, cut into 3-inch pieces

1 cup craft-brewed pale ale

1 cup barbecue sauce

1 teaspoon chili powder

4 (8-inch) flour tortillas

2⅔ cups shredded Monterey jack cheese

Salsa, sour cream and fresh cilantro (optional)

1. Combine pork, beer, barbecue sauce and chili powder in large saucepan over medium-high heat; bring to a boil. Reduce heat to medium-low. Cover; simmer 50 minutes or until pork is tender, stirring occasionally. Transfer pork to large bowl; shred using two forks.

2. Bring remaining sauce to a boil over medium-high heat. Boil 8 to 10 minutes or until thickened. Add ¾ cup sauce to shredded pork; discard remaining sauce.

3. Place tortillas on work surface. Layer bottom half of each tortilla evenly with cheese and pork. Fold top halves of tortillas over filling to form semicircle. Heat large nonstick skillet over medium heat. Cook two quesadillas at a time 6 to 8 minutes or until golden and cheese is melted, turning once. Cut into wedges.

4. Serve with salsa, sour cream and cilantro.

BEER-BATTERED MUSHROOMS

MAKES 6 TO 8 SERVINGS

1 cup all-purpose flour
½ teaspoon baking powder
½ teaspoon chili powder
¼ teaspoon salt, plus extra for seasoning
⅛ teaspoon black pepper
1 cup craft-brewed pilsner
1 egg, separated
  Vegetable oil
1 pound small mushrooms

1. Combine flour, baking powder, chili powder, salt and black pepper in medium bowl. Whisk beer and egg yolk in small bowl. Stir beer mixture into flour mixture just until blended.

2. Beat egg white in medium bowl with electric mixer at medium speed until soft peaks form. Fold egg white into beer mixture

3. Heat 1 inch of oil in large saucepan until it reaches 365°F; adjust heat to maintain temperature

4. Dip mushrooms into batter in batches and add to hot oil. Fry mushrooms until golden brown, turning occasionally. (Stir batter between batches.) Remove mushrooms to wire racks or paper towels to drain; immediately season with salt. Serve hot.

ONION PALE ALE DIP

MAKES 1½ CUPS DIP

8 ounces sour cream
3 tablespoons whipped cream cheese
3 tablespoons minced onion
1 teaspoon onion powder
¼ teaspoon salt
¼ cup craft-brewed pale ale
  Chips, bread slices and/or vegetables

Place sour cream, cream cheese, onion, onion powder, salt and beer in medium bowl. Mix just until combined. Refrigerate at least 30 minutes. Serve with chips, bread slices or vegetables.

CHICKEN WINGS IN CERVEZA
MAKES 6 SERVINGS

1½ pounds chicken wings or drummettes
1 teaspoon salt
1 teaspoon dried thyme
⅛ teaspoon black pepper
1 bottle (12 ounces) craft-brewed Vienna-style lager or light-colored lager

1. Cut off and discard wing tips. Cut each wing in half at joint. Place chicken in shallow bowl; sprinkle with salt, thyme and pepper. Pour beer over chicken; toss to coat. Cover and refrigerate 2 to 6 hours.

2. Preheat oven to 375°F. Line baking sheet with foil; spray with nonstick cooking spray.

3. Drain chicken, reserving marinade. Arrange chicken in single layer on prepared baking sheet. Bake 40 minutes or until chicken is cooked through and browned on all sides, turning and basting with reserved marinade occasionally. *Do not brush with marinade during last 5 minutes of baking.* Discard remaining marinade. Serve warm or at room temperature.

NOTE:
When using drummettes, simply place them in the marinade without cutting.

HOT CHEESE-CHIPOTLE DIP

MAKES 3 CUPS DIP

2 tablespoons butter

1 onion, chopped

½ red bell pepper, finely chopped

1 clove garlic, minced

2 tablespoons all-purpose flour

1 can (about 14 ounces) diced tomatoes, drained and 2 tablespoons juice reserved

1 cup craft-brewed Vienna-style lager or light-colored lager

1 canned chipotle pepper in adobo sauce, minced, plus 1 teaspoon adobo sauce

4 cups (16 ounces) shredded Mexican cheese blend

Chopped fresh cilantro (optional)

Tortilla chips

1. Melt butter in medium saucepan over medium heat. Add onion, bell pepper and garlic; cook and stir 5 minutes or until tender. Add flour; stir until well blended. Stir in tomatoes and reserved juice, lager, chipotle pepper and adobo sauce; bring to a boil. Reduce heat to low; simmer 5 minutes or until thickened.

2. Remove from heat. Stir in cheese, 1 cup at a time, until each addition is melted. If necessary, return to very low heat and stir just until melted. Garnish with cilantro. Serve warm with tortilla chips.

NOTE:
Do not overcook the cheese or it will become gritty.

★ Tip ★
For a zestier flavor, add more adobo
sauce from the canned chipotle.

COCONUT SHRIMP

MAKES 4 SERVINGS

Spicy Orange-Mustard Sauce (recipe follows)

¾ cup all-purpose flour

¾ cup craft-brewed pilsner

1 egg

¾ teaspoon baking powder

½ teaspoon salt

¼ teaspoon ground red pepper

1 cup flaked coconut

2 packages (3 ounces each) ramen noodles, any flavor,* crushed

20 jumbo raw shrimp, peeled and deveined (with tails on)

2 cups vegetable oil

*Discard seasoning packets.

1. Prepare Spicy Orange-Mustard Sauce; set aside.

2. Whisk flour, beer, egg, baking powder, salt and red pepper in medium bowl. Combine coconut and noodles in another medium bowl. Dip shrimp in beer batter; shake off excess. Coat with coconut mixture.

3. Heat oil in large skillet until it reaches 350°F. Cook shrimp in batches 3 minutes or just until golden, turning once halfway through cooking. Remove to wire racks or paper towels to drain. Serve with Spicy Orange-Mustard Sauce.

SPICY ORANGE-MUSTARD SAUCE:
Combine ¼ cup coarse grain or Dijon mustard, 2 tablespoons orange juice, 2 tablespoons honey, 2 teaspoons grated orange peel, ½ teaspoon ground red pepper and ¼ teaspoon ground ginger in small bowl until blended.

★ Tip ★

Use one hand to dip the shrimp in the beer batter and
the other hand to coat with coconut mixture. This way, your
hands will not mix up the mixtures and create a mess.

THICK POTATO CHIPS WITH BEER KETCHUP

MAKES 4 SERVINGS

Beer Ketchup (recipe follows)
Peanut oil
3 baking potatoes, scrubbed
Sea salt and black pepper

1. Prepare Beer Ketchup. Heat 2 inches of oil in deep saucepan until it reaches 345°F.

2. Slice potatoes into ¼-inch-thick slices. Add to hot oil in batches. Fry 2 minutes per side, flipping to brown evenly. Remove to wire rack or paper towels to drain; immediately sprinkle with salt and pepper.

3. Serve with Beer Ketchup.

BEER KETCHUP:

Combine ¾ cup ketchup, ¼ cup craft-brewed pilsner, 1 tablespoon Worcestershire sauce, ¼ teaspoon onion powder and ⅛ teaspoon ground red pepper in small saucepan. Bring to a boil over medium-high heat. Reduce heat to medium-low; simmer 2 to 3 minutes. Remove from heat and let cool. Cover and refrigerate until ready to use.

★ Tip ★

If the potatoes begin browning too quickly, turn down the heat
and wait for the oil to cool to the proper temperature. Too high a
temperature will not cook the potatoes completely, and too
low a temperature will make the chips soggy.

BEER-FA-LO WINGS WITH BLUE CHEESE DIP

MAKES 10 TO 12 SERVINGS

5 pounds chicken wings, tips removed and split at joint

1 tablespoon olive oil

1 cup craft-brewed lager

½ cup hot pepper sauce

1 teaspoon Worcestershire sauce

6 tablespoons butter

Blue Cheese Dip (recipe follows)

1. Preheat oven to 450°F. Spray baking sheets with nonstick cooking spray.

2. Combine wings and oil in large bowl; toss to coat. Arrange wings on prepared baking sheets in single layer. Bake 40 to 45 minutes or until crisp and cooked through, rotating baking sheets halfway through baking time.

3. Meanwhile, prepare Blue Cheese Dip.

4. Combine beer, hot pepper sauce and Worcestershire sauce in small saucepan. Bring to a boil over medium-high heat; boil 12 to 14 minutes or until reduced to ½ cup. Remove from heat; stir in butter until melted.

5. Transfer wings to another large bowl. Add beer mixture; toss to coat. Transfer to platter; serve with dip.

BLUE CHEESE DIP:
Combine 1 cup sour cream, ¾ cup blue cheese, ½ cup mayonnaise, 1 teaspoon vinegar, ¼ teaspoon salt and ⅛ teaspoon black pepper in small bowl; mix well. Refrigerate until ready to use.

LAYERED BEAN DIP

1 can (about 15 ounces) pinto beans, rinsed and drained

1 bottle (12 ounces) craft-brewed Vienna-style lager or light-colored lager

1½ cups chopped onions

3 cloves garlic, minced

2 teaspoons ground cumin

1 teaspoon salt

1 teaspoon dried oregano

1 cup guacamole

1 cup sour cream

1 cup salsa

½ cup chopped black olives

½ cup chopped green onions

1½ cups (6 ounces) shredded Cheddar or Monterey Jack cheese

Tortilla chips

1. Combine beans, beer, onions, garlic, cumin, salt and oregano in large saucepan. Simmer over low heat 15 minutes or until liquid has evaporated, stirring occasionally. Remove from heat. Mash with potato masher or process in food processor. Set aside to cool.

2. Spread half of cooled beans in large 2-inch deep dish or casserole. Top with half of guacamole, half of sour cream, half of salsa, half of olives and half of green onions. Repeat layers. Top with cheese. Serve with tortilla chips.

VARIATION:
Use refried beans instead of whole beans. Combine a 15-ounce can of refried beans and 6 ounces of beer in a small saucepan. If the beans are not seasoned, add garlic, cumin and oregano. Simmer about 10 minutes over low heat; let cool.

PEPPERONI PIZZA
MAKES 2 (10-INCH) PIZZAS

1 cup craft-brewed pale ale, at room temperature

3 tablespoons olive oil

1 package (¼ ounce) active dry yeast

2¾ cups bread flour, divided

1 teaspoon salt

6 ounces pepperoni slices (about 34)

1 cup prepared pizza sauce

2 cups (8 ounces) shredded mozzarella cheese

¼ cup freshly grated Parmesan cheese

1. Mix ale and oil in medium bowl; stir in yeast. Stir in 1 cup flour and salt. Gradually stir in enough flour to make thick dough. Turn dough out onto floured surface. Knead 8 minutes, adding enough remaining flour to make smooth and elastic dough.

2. Shape dough into a ball. Place in lightly greased medium bowl; turn to grease top. Cover with plastic wrap; let rise in warm place about 1 hour or until doubled in size.

3. Preheat oven to 425°F.

4. Divide dough in half. Shape into two balls. Place on lightly floured surface; cover with plastic wrap. Let stand 10 minutes. Roll out each ball into 10-inch round. Transfer to baking sheet. Spread each with ½ cup pizza sauce, leaving ½-inch border around edges. Top with pepperoni, mozzarella and Parmesan.

5. Bake 15 minutes or until crust is golden brown and cheese is bubbly. Let stand 3 minutes before serving.

ALTERNATE METHOD:

To make dough in a heavy-duty mixer, combine beer, oil and yeast in large mixer bowl. Add 1 cup flour and salt; mix on low speed with paddle blade, adding enough flour to make soft dough that cleans the bowl. Change to dough hook and knead on medium-low speed 8 minutes or until dough is soft, smooth and elastic, adding more flour if needed.

SOUPS & STEWS

OXTAIL SOUP WITH BEER
MAKES 4 SERVINGS

2½ pounds oxtails (beef or veal)
1 large onion, sliced
4 carrots, cut into 1-inch pieces, divided
3 stalks celery, cut into 1-inch pieces, divided
2 sprigs fresh parsley
5 whole black peppercorns
1 bay leaf
4 cups beef broth
1 cup craft-brewed brown ale
2 cups diced baking potatoes
1 teaspoon salt

1. Combine oxtails, onion, half of carrots, one third of celery, parsley, peppercorns and bay leaf in large saucepan. Add broth and beer; bring to a boil. Reduce heat to low; cover and simmer 3 hours or until meat is falling off bones.

2. Remove oxtails; set aside. Strain broth and return to saucepan; skim fat. Add remaining carrots, celery and potatoes; bring to a simmer. Cook 10 to 15 minutes or until vegetables are tender.

3. Remove meat from oxtails and add to saucepan with salt; heat through. Ladle soup into bowls.

CHICKEN AND SAUSAGE GUMBO WITH BEER

MAKES 6 SERVINGS

½ cup all-purpose flour

½ cup vegetable oil

4½ cups chicken broth

1 bottle (12 ounces) craft-brewed pilsner

3 pounds boneless skinless chicken thighs

1½ teaspoons salt, divided

½ teaspoon garlic powder

¾ teaspoon ground red pepper, divided

1 pound fully cooked andouille sausage, sliced into rounds

1 large onion, chopped

½ red bell pepper, chopped

½ green bell pepper, chopped

2 stalks celery, chopped

2 cloves garlic, minced

2 bay leaves

½ teaspoon black pepper

3 cups hot cooked rice

½ cup sliced green onions

1 teaspoon filé powder (optional)

1. Whisk together flour and oil in large saucepan or Dutch oven. Cook over medium-low heat 20 minutes or until mixture is caramel colored, whisking continuously. (Once mixture begins to darken, watch carefully to avoid burning.)

2. Meanwhile, bring broth and beer to a simmer in medium saucepan over medium heat. Keep warm over low heat. Season chicken with ½ teaspoon salt, garlic powder and ¼ teaspoon ground red pepper.

3. Add chicken, sausage, onion, bell peppers, celery, garlic, bay leaves, remaining 1 teaspoon salt, black pepper and remaining ½ teaspoon ground red pepper to Dutch oven; stir well. Gradually add hot broth mixture, whisking constantly to prevent lumps. Bring to a simmer. Cover and simmer 1 to 2 hours.

4. Remove and discard bay leaves. Place ½ cup rice in each of six bowls; top with gumbo. Sprinkle with green onions and filé powder, if desired, before serving.

DURANGO CHILI

MAKES 6 SERVINGS

3 tablespoons vegetable oil, divided

1 pound ground beef

1 pound boneless beef top sirloin steak, cut into ½-inch pieces

2 onions, chopped

1 green bell pepper, chopped

4 cloves garlic, minced

2 cans (about 14 ounces each) diced tomatoes

1 bottle (12 ounces) craft-brewed porter or brown ale

1 can (10¾ ounces) condensed beef broth plus 1 can water

2 cans (4 ounces each) diced green chiles, undrained

3 to 5 jalapeño peppers,* seeded and minced

5 tablespoons chili powder

¼ cup tomato paste

2 bay leaves

1 teaspoon salt

1 teaspoon ground cumin

½ teaspoon black pepper

2 cans (about 15 ounces each) pinto or kidney beans, rinsed and drained

Shredded Cheddar cheese

Sliced green onions

Jalapeño peppers can sting and irritate the skin, so wear rubber gloves when handling peppers and do not touch your eyes.

1. Heat 1 tablespoon oil in large saucepan or Dutch oven over medium-high heat. Brown ground beef, stirring to break up meat. Add steak; cook until meat is browned, stirring occasionally. Drain fat. Transfer meat to medium bowl.

2. Heat remaining 2 tablespoons oil in saucepan over medium heat. Add onions, bell pepper and garlic; cook and stir 5 minutes or until tender. Return meat to saucepan. Stir in tomatoes, beer, broth, water, chiles, jalapeño peppers, chili powder, tomato paste, bay leaves, salt, cumin and black pepper. Bring to a boil. Reduce heat to low; simmer, partially covered, 2 hours or until meat is very tender. Stir in beans. Simmer, uncovered, until heated through. Remove and discard bay leaves. Top with cheese and green onions.

BEER AND CHEESE SOUP

MAKES 6 SERVINGS

2 to 3 slices pumpernickel or rye bread

3 tablespoons water

3 tablespoons cornstarch

1 tablespoon butter

¼ cup finely chopped onion

2 cloves garlic, minced

¾ teaspoon dried thyme

1 can (about 14 ounces) vegetable or chicken broth

1½ cups (6 ounces) shredded American cheese

1 to 1½ cups (4 to 6 ounces) shredded sharp Cheddar cheese

1 cup craft-brewed pilsner

½ teaspoon paprika

1 cup milk

1. Preheat oven to 425°F. Cut bread into ½-inch cubes; place on ungreased baking sheet. Bake 10 to 12 minutes or until crisp, stirring once; set aside.

2. Meanwhile, stir water into cornstarch in small bowl until smooth. Melt butter in medium saucepan oven medium-high heat. Add onion, garlic and thyme; cook and stir 3 to 4 minutes or until onion is tender. Add broth; bring to a boil. Stir in cheeses, beer and paprika. Reduce heat to low; whisk in milk and cornstarch mixture. Stir until cheese melts and soup bubbles and thickens. Ladle into bowls. Top with croutons.

MING DYNASTY BEEF STEW
MAKES 6 TO 8 SERVINGS

2 pounds boneless beef chuck or veal shoulder, cut into 1½-inch pieces

1 teaspoon Chinese five-spice powder

½ teaspoon red pepper flakes

2 tablespoons peanut or vegetable oil

1 large onion, coarsely chopped

2 cloves garlic, minced

1 cup beef broth

1 cup craft-brewed Japanese-style rice lager

2 tablespoons soy sauce

1 tablespoon cornstarch

Hot cooked rice noodles

OPTIONAL TOPPINGS

Grated lemon peel, chopped peanuts and/or chopped fresh cilantro

1. Sprinkle beef with five-spice powder and red pepper flakes. Heat 1 tablespoon oil in large saucepan or Dutch oven over medium-high heat. Brown beef in batches, adding additional oil as needed. Remove from saucepan.

2. Add onion and garlic to saucepan; cook 3 minutes or until onion is tender, stirring occasionally. Add broth and beer; bring to a boil. Reduce heat to medium-low. Return beef along with any accumulated juices to saucepan; cover and simmer 1 hour 15 minutes or until beef is fork-tender.*

3. Stir soy sauce into cornstarch in small bowl until smooth. Stir into saucepan. Cook, uncovered, 2 minutes or until mixture thickens, stirring occasionally. Serve over rice noodles. Garnish with lemon peel, peanuts and cilantro.

Stew may be oven-braised in ovenproof saucepan or Dutch oven. Cover and bake in 350°F oven 1 hour 15 minutes or until beef is fork-tender. Proceed as directed in step 3.

CHICKEN AND BEER DUMPLINGS
MAKES 6 SERVINGS

1¾ cups all-purpose flour, divided

1½ teaspoons salt, divided

1 cut-up whole chicken (about 4 pounds)

3 tablespoons canola oil

1 cup chopped onion

¾ cup chopped carrot

¾ cup chopped celery

2 cloves garlic, minced

1 bay leaf

½ teaspoon thyme

4 cups chicken broth

2 teaspoons baking powder

2 teaspoons sugar

¾ cup craft-brewed pilsner

3 tablespoons chopped fresh parsley

1. Combine ¼ cup flour and ½ teaspoon salt in large bowl. Add chicken; toss well to coat.

2. Heat oil in Dutch oven over medium-high heat. Cook chicken in batches 10 minutes or until browned on all sides. Transfer chicken to plate and keep warm. Add onion, carrot, celery, garlic, bay leaf and thyme to Dutch oven; cook 3 to 4 minutes or until vegetables start to soften, stirring occasionally. Add broth, chicken and ½ teaspoon salt; bring to a boil. Reduce heat to medium-low; cover and simmer 30 minutes.

3. Meanwhile, combine remaining 1½ cups flour, baking powder, sugar and remaining ½ teaspoon salt in large bowl. Stir in beer and parsley just until moistened. Drop mixture in 12 mounds on top of chicken mixture. Cover and return to a simmer. Cook 9 to 10 minutes or until toothpick inserted into centers of dumplings comes out clean. Remove and discard bay leaf.

BEEF CHUCK CHILI

MAKES 8 TO 10 SERVINGS

3 tablespoons olive oil

5 pounds beef chuck roast, trimmed of fat

3 cups minced onions

4 poblano peppers,* diced

2 serrano peppers,* diced

2 green bell peppers, diced

3 jalapeño peppers, diced

2 tablespoons minced garlic

1 can (28 ounces) crushed tomatoes

½ cup craft-brewed Vienna-style lager or light-colored lager

¼ cup hot pepper sauce

1 tablespoon ground cumin

Black pepper

Corn bread or hot cooked rice

If fresh poblano or serrano peppers are unavailable, use 2 cans (4 ounces each) diced green chiles and add ground red pepper for more heat.

SLOW COOKER DIRECTIONS

1. Heat oil in large skillet over medium-high heat. Add roast; brown on all sides. Transfer to slow cooker.

2. Add onions, peppers and garlic to skillet; cook and stir 5 minutes or until onions are tender. Transfer to slow cooker. Stir in crushed tomatoes. Cover; cook on LOW 4 to 5 hours or until beef is fork-tender.

3. Shred beef. Stir in beer, hot pepper sauce and cumin. Season with black pepper. Serve over corn bread.

FARMER'S MARKET GRILLED CHOWDER

MAKES 4 SERVINGS

1 ear corn

1 large potato

1 small zucchini, cut lengthwise into ¼-inch-thick slices

1 tablespoon butter

½ cup chopped onion

2 tablespoons all-purpose flour

½ teaspoon salt

½ teaspoon dried thyme

⅛ teaspoon white pepper

1 cup craft-brewed wheat beer

1 cup milk

½ cup (2 ounces) shredded sharp Cheddar cheese

1. Prepare grill for direct cooking. Remove husks and silk from corn. Cut potato in half lengthwise. Grill corn and potato, covered, 20 minutes or until tender, turning once. Remove kernels from cob. Cut potato into cubes. Set aside.

2. Spray zucchini with nonstick cooking spray. Grill, uncovered, 4 minutes or until tender, turning once. Cut into bite-size pieces; set aside.

3. Melt butter in large saucepan over medium heat. Add onion; cook and stir 5 minutes or until tender. Stir in flour, salt, thyme and white pepper; cook and stir 1 minute.

4. Stir beer and milk into flour mixture. Bring to a boil. Reduce heat to medium-low; simmer 1 minute. Stir in corn, potato, zucchini and cheese. Simmer until heated through, stirring constantly.

CHILE VERDE CHICKEN STEW
MAKES 6 SERVINGS

⅓ cup all-purpose flour

1½ teaspoons salt, divided

¼ teaspoon black pepper

1½ pounds boneless skinless chicken breasts, cut into 1½-inch pieces

4 tablespoons vegetable oil, divided

1 pound tomatillos (about 9), husked and halved

2 onions, chopped

2 cans (4 ounces each) mild green chiles

1 tablespoon dried oregano

1 tablespoon ground cumin

2 cloves garlic, chopped

1 teaspoon sugar

2 cups chicken broth

1 cup craft-brewed Vienna-style lager or light-colored lager

5 red potatoes, diced

OPTIONAL TOPPINGS

Chopped fresh cilantro, sour cream, shredded Cheddar cheese, lime wedges, diced avocado and/or hot pepper sauce

1. Combine flour, 1 teaspoon salt and pepper in large bowl. Add chicken; toss to coat. Heat 2 tablespoons oil in large nonstick skillet over medium heat. Add chicken; cook until lightly browned on all sides, stirring occasionally. Transfer to large saucepan or Dutch oven.

2. Heat remaining 2 tablespoons oil in same skillet. Stir in tomatillos, onions, chiles, oregano, cumin, garlic, sugar and remaining ½ teaspoon salt. Cook and stir 20 minutes or until vegetables are softened. Stir in broth and beer. Remove from heat. Working in batches, process mixture in food processor or blender until almost smooth.

3. Add mixture to chicken in saucepan. Stir in potatoes. Cover; bring to a boil over medium-high heat. Reduce heat to low; simmer 1 hour or until potatoes are tender, stirring occasionally. Serve with desired toppings.

VARIATION:

Omit potatoes and serve over rice.

BEER-BRAISED CHILI

MAKES ABOUT 8 SERVINGS

2 tablespoons canola or vegetable oil

2 pounds boneless beef chuck roast or stew meat, cut into ¾-inch pieces

1 large onion, chopped

4 cloves garlic, minced

1 tablespoon chili powder

1 tablespoon ground cumin

1¼ teaspoons salt

1 teaspoon dried oregano

½ teaspoon ground red pepper

1 can (about 14 ounces) Mexican-style stewed tomatoes, undrained

1 bottle (12 ounces) craft-brewed India pale ale

½ cup salsa

1 can (about 15 ounces) black beans, rinsed and drained

1 can (about 15 ounces) red beans or pinto beans, rinsed and drained

OPTIONAL TOPPINGS

Chopped cilantro, thinly sliced green onions, shredded Chihuahua and/or Cheddar cheese, sliced pickled jalapeño peppers, sour cream

1. Heat oil in large saucepan or Dutch oven over medium-high heat. Add beef, onion and garlic; cook 5 minutes, stirring occasionally. Sprinkle chili powder, cumin, salt, oregano and ground red pepper over mixture; mix well. Add tomatoes, beer and salsa; bring to a boil. Reduce heat to low; cover and simmer 1¼ hours or until beef is very tender, stirring once.

2. Stir in beans. Simmer, uncovered, 20 minutes or until thickened. Serve with desired toppings.

JAMBALAYA

MAKES 6 TO 8 SERVINGS

1 package (16 ounces) andouille sausage, sliced

1 cup chopped onion

1 cup chopped green bell pepper

½ cup chopped celery

2 cloves garlic, minced

2 cups uncooked rice

2 cups chicken broth

1 bottle (12 ounces) craft-brewed pale ale or other light-colored beer

1 can (about 14 ounces) diced tomatoes with green pepper, onion and celery

1 teaspoon Cajun seasoning

1 pound medium cooked shrimp, peeled and deveined

Chopped fresh parsley (optional)

Hot pepper sauce (optional)

1. Brown sausage in large saucepan or Dutch oven over medium-high heat; drain fat. Add onion, bell pepper, celery and garlic; cook and stir 2 to 3 minutes or until tender. Add rice, broth and beer. Cover; bring to a boil. Reduce heat to low. Simmer 20 minutes, stirring occasionally.

2. Stir tomatoes and Cajun seasoning into saucepan; cook 5 minutes. Add shrimp; cook 2 to 3 minutes or until heated through. Sprinkle with parsley and hot pepper sauce, if desired.

BAKING WITH BEER

FIESTA BREAD
MAKES 8 SERVINGS

½ pound chorizo sausage, casings removed

½ cup chopped onion

1¼ cups all-purpose flour

1 cup cornmeal

1½ teaspoons baking soda

1 teaspoon ground cumin

½ teaspoon salt

1 cup craft-brewed Vienna-style lager or light-colored lager

1 cup (4 ounces) shredded Cheddar cheese

1 can (4 ounces) diced mild green chiles, drained

1 egg, beaten

1. Preheat oven to 375°F. Grease 8-inch square baking pan. Brown sausage and onion in medium skillet over medium-high heat, stirring to break up meat. Drain fat.

2. Combine flour, cornmeal, baking soda, cumin and salt in large bowl. Combine beer, cheese, chiles and egg in medium bowl. Add to flour mixture; stir just until moistened. Stir in chorizo mixture. Spread in prepared pan.

3. Bake 20 minutes or until toothpick inserted into center comes out clean. Cool in pan 10 minutes. Serve warm. Refrigerate leftovers.

SOFT BEER PRETZELS
MAKES 1 DOZEN PRETZELS

3¼ cups all-purpose flour, divided

1 package (¼ ounce) rapid-rise active dry yeast

1 teaspoon kosher salt, plus additional for serving

6½ cups water, divided

⅔ cup craft-brewed pilsner or lager

2 tablespoons vegetable oil

2 tablespoons baking soda

1 egg, beaten

1. Combine 3 cups flour, yeast and 1 teaspoon salt in large bowl. Heat ½ cup water, beer and oil in small saucepan to 120°F. Add to flour mixture; beat with electric mixer at low speed until moistened. Stir in remaining ¼ cup flour, 1 tablespoon at a time, until soft dough forms. Turn dough out onto lightly floured surface; knead 5 to 6 minutes or until smooth and elastic. Cover and let rise in warm place 15 minutes.

2. Divide dough in half; cut each half into 6 pieces. Roll each piece into 14-inch rope with lightly floured hands. (Keep remaining dough covered with kitchen towel to prevent it from drying out.) Twist each rope into pretzel shape, pressing edges to seal. Place on greased baking sheets. Cover and let rise in warm place 15 minutes.

3. Preheat oven to 400°F. Spray wire rack with nonstick cooking spray; place on baking sheet. Bring 6 cups water to a boil in large saucepan; stir in baking soda. Working in batches, gently lower pretzels into boiling water; cook 30 seconds, turning once. Use slotted spoon to remove pretzels to prepared wire rack.

4. Brush pretzels with egg and sprinkle with salt. Bake 10 minutes or until golden brown. Cool on wire rack.

TIP:

When shaping pretzels, make large exaggerated loops. Smaller loops will close when boiled.

CHEDDAR-BEER HUSH PUPPIES
MAKES ABOUT 3 DOZEN HUSH PUPPIES

1½ cups medium grain cornmeal

1 cup all-purpose flour

2 tablespoons sugar

1 teaspoon baking powder

1 teaspoon baking soda

1 teaspoon salt

¼ teaspoon black pepper

1 bottle (12 ounces) craft-brewed lager

1 egg, beaten

¾ cup (3 ounces) shredded Cheddar cheese

2 jalapeño peppers,* seeded and minced

Vegetable oil

Jalapeño peppers can sting and irritate the skin, so wear rubber gloves when handling peppers and do not touch your eyes.

1. Whisk cornmeal, flour, sugar, baking powder, baking soda, salt and black pepper in large bowl. Whisk beer and egg until combined in medium bowl. Gradually whisk beer mixture into cornmeal mixture until smooth. Stir in cheese and jalapeños.

2. Heat 3 inches of oil in large saucepan until it reaches 350°F. Line baking sheet with three layers of paper towels.

3. Working in batches, drop heaping tablespoonfuls of batter into hot oil. Fry 2 minutes or until golden brown, turning occasionally. Transfer to prepared baking sheet to drain. Serve immediately.

BACON AND CHEESE MUFFINS
MAKES 1 DOZEN MUFFINS

6 slices bacon, chopped

2 cups chopped onions

3 teaspoons sugar, divided

¼ teaspoon dried thyme

1½ cups all-purpose flour

¾ cup grated Parmesan cheese

2 teaspoons baking powder

½ teaspoon salt

¾ cup craft-brewed lager

2 eggs

¼ cup extra virgin olive oil

1. Preheat oven to 375°F. Grease 12 standard (2½-inch) muffin cups.

2. Cook bacon in large skillet over medium heat until crisp, stirring occasionally. Remove bacon to paper towel-lined plate with slotted spoon. Add onions, 1 teaspoon sugar and thyme to skillet; cook 12 minutes or until onions are golden brown, stirring occasionally. Cool 5 minutes; stir in bacon.

3. Combine flour, cheese, baking powder, remaining 2 teaspoons sugar and salt in large bowl. Whisk lager, eggs and oil in medium bowl. Add to flour mixture; stir just until moistened. Gently stir in onion mixture. Spoon batter evenly into prepared muffin cups.

4. Bake 15 minutes or until toothpick inserted into centers comes out clean. Cool in pan 5 minutes. Serve warm or at room temperature. Refrigerate leftovers.

GINGERBREAD WITH LEMON SAUCE

MAKES 9 SERVINGS

2½ cups all-purpose flour

1½ teaspoons ground cinnamon

1 teaspoon ground ginger

½ teaspoon baking soda

½ teaspoon salt

½ cup (1 stick) butter, softened

¾ cup packed brown sugar

⅓ cup light molasses

1 egg

¾ cup craft-brewed stout, at room temperature

Lemon Sauce (recipe follows)

Grated lemon peel (optional)

1. Preheat oven to 350°F. Grease bottom of 9-inch square baking pan. Combine flour, cinnamon, ginger, baking soda and salt in medium bowl.

2. Beat butter and brown sugar in large bowl with electric mixer at medium speed until light and fluffy. Add molasses and egg; beat well. Add flour mixture one third at a time, alternating with stout, beginning and ending with flour mixture and beating after each addition. Pour batter evenly into prepared pan.

3. Bake 35 to 40 minutes or until toothpick inserted into center comes out clean. Cool completely in pan on wire rack. Prepare Lemon Sauce.

4. Cut cake into 9 squares. Top each cake square with sauce and sprinkle with grated lemon peel, if desired.

LEMON SAUCE:

Combine 1 cup granulated sugar, ¾ cup whipping cream and ½ cup (1 stick) butter in small saucepan. Cook over medium heat until butter is melted, stirring constantly. Reduce heat to low; simmer 5 minutes. Stir in 1 tablespoon lemon juice and 2 teaspoons grated lemon peel. Cool slightly.

CHERRY SCONES
MAKES 8 SCONES

1½ cups all-purpose flour

1 cup whole wheat flour

3 tablespoons granulated sugar

2 teaspoons baking powder

¼ teaspoon salt

½ cup shortening

½ cup craft-brewed honey beer

⅓ cup milk

1 egg, beaten

¾ cup dried cherries

1 teaspoon raw sugar

1. Preheat oven to 425°F.

2. Combine flours, granulated sugar, baking powder and salt in large bowl. Cut in shortening with pastry blender or two knives until mixture resembles coarse crumbs. Whisk beer, milk and egg in medium bowl. Add to flour mixture; stir just until moistened. Stir in cherries. Knead gently on floured surface four times.

3. Shape dough into ball; place on ungreased baking sheet. Pat into 8-inch circle. Score dough into 8 wedges (do not separate). Sprinkle with raw sugar.

4. Bake 18 minutes or until golden brown. Cut into wedges.

MUSTARD BEER BISCUITS

MAKES ABOUT 1 DOZEN BISCUITS

2 cups all-purpose flour

2 teaspoons baking powder

¾ teaspoon salt

¼ cup shortening

¼ cup (½ stick) cold butter

½ cup craft-brewed pilsner

1 tablespoon plus 1 teaspoon yellow mustard, divided

1 tablespoon milk

1. Preheat oven to 425°F. Grease large baking sheet.

2. Combine flour, baking powder and salt in large bowl. Cut in shortening and butter with pastry blender or two knives until mixture resembles coarse crumbs. Whisk beer and 1 tablespoon mustard in small bowl. Add to flour mixture; stir just until moistened. Knead gently on floured surface eight times.

3. Pat dough to ½-inch thickness. Cut out biscuits with 2-inch round cutter. Reroll scraps and cut out additional biscuits. Place 1 inch apart on prepared baking sheet. Combine remaining 1 teaspoon mustard with milk in small bowl. Brush over tops of biscuits.

4. Bake 13 minutes or until lightly browned. Remove to wire rack to cool slightly.

BEER PRETZEL ROLLS
MAKES 12 ROLLS

1¼ cups craft-brewed lager or pale ale, at room temperature

3 tablespoons brown sugar

2 tablespoons milk

2 tablespoons butter, melted

1 package (¼ ounce) rapid-rise active dry yeast

3 to 4 cups bread flour

2 teaspoons salt

4 quarts (16 cups) water

½ cup baking soda

2 teaspoons kosher salt

1. Combine lager, brown sugar, milk, butter and yeast in medium bowl. Stir in 2 cups flour and salt. Gradually stir in enough remaining flour to make stiff dough. Turn dough out onto lightly floured surface. Knead 8 minutes, adding enough remaining flour to make smooth and elastic dough. Shape dough into ball; place in lightly greased large bowl. Turn to grease top. Cover with plastic wrap and let rise in warm place 1 hour or until doubled in size.

2. Turn out dough onto lightly floured surface; knead briefly. Shape into 12 equal pieces. Shape each into smooth ball by gently pulling top surface to underside; pinch bottom to seal. Place on ungreased baking sheet. Cover with plastic wrap; let rise in warm place 30 minutes or until doubled in size.

3. Position oven rack in center of oven. Preheat oven to 425°F. Grease second baking sheet.

4. Bring water and baking soda to a boil in large saucepan. Add rolls to water a few at a time; cook about 30 seconds or until puffed, turning once. Drain rolls on clean kitchen towel. Place rolls on prepared baking sheet 2 inches apart. Cut 1½-inch X in top of each roll using kitchen shears. Sprinkle with kosher salt.

5. Bake 15 to 18 minutes or until browned. Remove from baking sheet; cool on wire rack.

ALTERNATE METHOD:
To make in a heavy-duty mixer, stir lager, brown sugar, milk, butter and yeast in large bowl. Add 1 cup flour and salt. Mix on low speed with paddle blade, adding enough flour to make stiff dough that cleans the bowl. Change to dough hook and knead on medium-low speed 8 minutes or until smooth and slightly tacky, adding more flour as needed.

GINGERBREAD STOUT CUPCAKES
MAKES 1 DOZEN CUPCAKES

CUPCAKES
1¼ cups all-purpose flour

1 teaspoon ground ginger

1 teaspoon ground cinnamon

¾ teaspoon baking soda

¼ teaspoon salt

½ cup (1 stick) butter, softened

½ cup packed brown sugar

1 egg

⅓ cup molasses (not blackstrap)

½ cup flat craft-brewed stout,* at room temperature

FROSTING
1½ cups powdered sugar, sifted

¼ cup (½ stick) butter, softened

3 tablespoons flat craft-brewed stout,* at room temperature

¼ cup finely chopped crystallized ginger

To flatten beer, open at least 1 hour before using.

1. Preheat oven to 350°F. Line 12 standard (2½-inch) muffin cups with paper baking cups.

2. For cupcakes, combine flour, ground ginger, cinnamon, baking soda and salt in large bowl. Beat butter in medium bowl with electric mixer at high speed 1 minute or until smooth. Add brown sugar; beat 3 minutes or until light and fluffy. Beat in egg and molasses. Reduce speed to low. Add flour mixture in three additions, alternately with stout, beginning and ending with flour mixture and beating after each addition until smooth. Spoon batter into prepared muffin cups, filling two-thirds full; smooth tops.

3. Bake 20 minutes or until toothpick inserted into centers comes out clean. Cool in pan 5 minutes. Remove to wire rack; cool completely.

4. For frosting, beat powdered sugar and butter in medium bowl with electric mixer at low speed until crumbly. Gradually beat in enough stout to make spreadable frosting. Stir in crystallized ginger. Frost cupcakes.

JALAPEÑO AND PALE ALE
CORN BREAD WITH HONEY BUTTER
MAKES 12 SERVINGS

1½ cups all-purpose flour

1½ cups yellow cornmeal

⅓ cup sugar

2 teaspoons baking powder

¾ teaspoon salt

½ teaspoon baking soda

1 cup craft-brewed pale ale

½ cup corn oil

½ cup buttermilk

2 eggs

2 jalapeño peppers,* finely chopped

Honey Butter (recipe follows)

Jalapeño peppers can sting and irritate the skin, so wear rubber gloves when handling peppers and do not touch your eyes.

1. Preheat oven to 400°F. Butter 8-inch square baking pan.

2. Combine flour, cornmeal, sugar, baking powder, salt and baking soda in large bowl. Whisk ale, oil, buttermilk, eggs and jalapeño peppers in medium bowl. Add to flour mixture; stir just until moistened. Pour batter into prepared pan.

3. Bake 25 to 27 minutes or until toothpick inserted into center comes out clean. Cool in pan 10 minutes. Meanwhile, prepare Honey Butter.

4. Cut corn bread into squares and serve warm with Honey Butter.

HONEY BUTTER:
Combine 6 tablespoons softened butter, 2 tablespoons honey and ¼ teaspoon salt in small bowl; stir until smooth.

BOSTON BROWN BREAD MUFFINS
MAKES 1 DOZEN MUFFINS

½ cup rye flour

½ cup whole wheat flour

½ cup yellow cornmeal

1½ teaspoons baking soda

¾ teaspoon salt

1 cup golden raisins

1 cup buttermilk

⅓ cup packed dark brown sugar

⅓ cup craft-brewed porter or brown ale

⅓ cup molasses

1 egg

Softened cream cheese

1. Preheat oven to 400°F. Grease 12 standard (2½-inch) muffin cups or line with paper baking cups.

2. Combine flours, cornmeal, baking soda and salt in large bowl; stir in raisins. Whisk buttermilk, brown sugar, beer, molasses and egg in another large bowl. Add to flour mixture; stir just until moistened. Spoon batter into prepared muffin cups, filling three-fourths full.

3. Bake 15 minutes or until toothpick inserted into centers comes out clean. Serve with cream cheese.

SOUR CREAM AND ONION ROLLS
MAKES 1 DOZEN ROLLS

    1 tablespoon butter

    1 cup chopped onion

3¼ cups all-purpose flour, divided

    1 package (¼ ounce) rapid-rise active dry yeast

    1 tablespoon sugar

    1 teaspoon salt

    1 cup warm craft-brewed lager

    ½ cup sour cream

    2 tablespoons butter, melted

1. Grease 10-inch pie plate. Melt 1 tablespoon butter in small skillet over medium-high heat. Add onion; cook and stir 3 to 4 minutes or until tender.

2. Combine 2 cups flour, yeast, sugar and salt in large bowl. Stir warm beer into flour mixture. Add sour cream; beat with electric mixer at high speed 2 minutes.

3. Stir in ½ cup onion. Stir in enough remaining flour to make soft dough. Shape into 12 equal balls with greased hands. Shape each into smooth ball by gently pulling top surface to underside; pinch bottom to seal. Place in prepared pie plate. Cover loosely with plastic wrap and let rise in warm place 20 minutes.

4. Preheat oven to 400°F. Brush tops of rolls with melted butter and sprinkle with remaining onion. Bake 25 to 30 minutes or until lightly browned.

PEPPERONI CHEESE BREAD
MAKES 2 (12-INCH) LOAVES

1 cup warm craft-brewed pilsner

½ cup warm milk

1 package (¼ ounce) active dry yeast

2¼ cups all-purpose flour, divided

1 cup rye flour

1 tablespoon dried basil

1 teaspoon sugar

1 teaspoon salt

1 teaspoon red pepper flakes

1 cup (4 ounces) shredded sharp Cheddar cheese

1 cup finely chopped pepperoni

1 tablespoon olive oil

1. Combine beer and milk in large bowl. Stir in yeast until dissolved. Stir in 2 cups all-purpose flour, rye flour, basil, sugar, salt and red pepper flakes until smooth. Stir in enough remaining all-purpose flour to form stiff dough. Turn dough out onto floured surface; sprinkle with cheese and pepperoni. Knead 5 to 6 minutes or until smooth and elastic. Transfer to greased bowl; turn to grease top. Cover with plastic wrap and let rise in warm place 1 hour or until doubled in size.

2. Punch dough down; divide in half. Shape into two 12-inch loaves. Place on greased baking sheets. Cover and let rise in warm place about 45 minutes or until doubled in size.

3. Preheat oven to 350°F. Bake bread 30 to 35 minutes or until golden brown. Brush with oil.

SERVING SUGGESTION:
Serve bread with an oregano-infused dipping oil. Combine 2 tablespoons olive oil, 1 tablespoon chopped green olives, ½ teaspoon black pepper and 1 sprig fresh oregano. Let stand several hours before serving to allow flavors to blend.

CHOCOLATE-RASPBERRY BEER BROWNIES
MAKES 16 SERVINGS

10 tablespoons butter, cut into pieces

4 ounces unsweetened chocolate, chopped

1 cup all-purpose flour

½ teaspoon baking powder

¼ teaspoon salt

1½ cups sugar

3 eggs

½ cup craft-brewed Belgian-style wit (white ale), at room temperature

2 teaspoons vanilla

½ cup seedless raspberry jam, stirred until smooth

1. Preheat oven to 350°F. Grease and flour 9-inch square baking pan.

2. Combine butter and chocolate in small saucepan; cook and stir over low heat until melted. Transfer to large bowl; cool 5 minutes.

3. Combine flour, baking powder and salt in medium bowl. Whisk sugar, eggs, ale and vanilla in another medium bowl. Stir ale mixture into chocolate mixture until well blended. Fold in flour mixture just until moistened. Pour batter into prepared baking pan; drizzle with raspberry jam.

4. Bake 30 to 35 minutes or until toothpick inserted into center comes out with moist crumbs attached. Cool completely in pan on wire rack. Cut into bars.

ROSEMARY LAGER FOCACCIA
MAKES 12 SERVINGS

1¼ cups craft-brewed lager
4 tablespoons extra virgin olive oil, divided
1 package (¼ ounce) active dry yeast
1 tablespoon sugar
3¼ cups all-purpose flour, divided
2 teaspoons kosher salt, divided
¼ cup fresh rosemary leaves

1. Place lager in medium microwavable bowl; microwave on HIGH 25 seconds. Stir in 3 tablespoons oil, yeast and sugar; let stand 5 minutes or until foamy.

2. Combine 3 cups flour and 1 teaspoon salt in large bowl. Stir lager mixture into flour mixture until dough pulls away from sides of bowl. Turn dough out onto floured surface; knead until smooth, elastic and slightly sticky, adding remaining flour 1 tablespoon at a time as necessary. Transfer to large greased bowl; turn to grease top. Cover with plastic wrap and let rise in warm place 1½ hours or until doubled in size.

3. Preheat oven to 325°F. Grease baking sheet.

4. Place dough on prepared baking sheet. Stretch into 15×10-inch rectangle. Cover; let stand 30 minutes.

5. Brush dough with remaining 1 tablespoon oil. Sprinkle with rosemary and remaining 1 teaspoon salt. Dimple with fingers or handle of wooden spoon. Bake 30 minutes or until golden brown. Cool 10 minutes before slicing. Serve warm or at room temperature.

NOTE:
To reheat, wrap leftovers in foil and warm 10 minutes in a 300°F oven before serving.

BEEF & BREW

BEST BEEF BRISKET SANDWICH EVER
MAKES 10 TO 12 SERVINGS

1 beef brisket (about 3 pounds)

2 cups apple cider, divided

⅓ cup chopped fresh thyme *or* 2 tablespoons dried thyme

1 head garlic, cloves separated and crushed

2 tablespoons whole black peppercorns

1 tablespoon mustard seeds

1 tablespoon Cajun seasoning

1 teaspoon ground cumin

1 teaspoon celery seed

1 teaspoon ground allspice

2 to 4 whole cloves

1 bottle (12 ounces) craft-brewed porter or brown ale

10 to 12 sourdough sandwich rolls, halved

SLOW COOKER DIRECTIONS

1. Place brisket, ½ cup cider, thyme, garlic, peppercorns, mustard seeds, Cajun seasoning, cumin, celery seed, allspice and cloves in large resealable food storage bag. Seal bag; turn to coat. Marinate in refrigerator overnight.

2. Place brisket and marinade in slow cooker. Add remaining 1½ cups cider and beer. Cover; cook on LOW 10 hours or until brisket is tender.

3. Slice brisket and place on sandwich rolls. Strain sauce; drizzle over meat.

SERVING SUGGESTION:
Add a mustard spread (page 18) or horseradish sauce to these sandwiches for extra flavor.

RUSTIC BEEF AND ALE RAGOÛT
MAKES 6 SERVINGS

1 tablespoon extra virgin olive oil

1½ pounds boneless beef chuck roast, cut into 1½-inch cubes

1 yellow onion, cut into ½-inch wedges

1 cup sliced carrots (about ¼-inch slices)

1 green bell pepper, sliced

1 bottle (12 ounces) craft-brewed pale ale or India pale ale

1 can (6 ounces) tomato paste

1 package (about 1 ounce) Italian salad dressing mix

2 teaspoons beef bouillon granules

2 teaspoons Worcestershire sauce

1 teaspoon sugar

Salt and black pepper

SLOW COOKER DIRECTIONS

1. Coat slow cooker with nonstick cooking spray.

2. Heat oil in large skillet over medium-high heat. Working in batches, brown beef on all sides. Transfer to slow cooker. Add onion, carrots and bell pepper to slow cooker.

3. Return skillet to medium-high heat. Whisk in beer, tomato paste, salad dressing mix, bouillon granules, Worcestershire sauce and sugar. Whisk until smooth, scraping up any browned bits from bottom of skillet. Pour over beef and vegetables in slow cooker; mix well. Cover; cook on HIGH 4 hours or until beef is tender. Season with salt and black pepper.

SERVING SUGGESTION:
For an even heartier meal, try serving this dish over mashed potatoes.

BEER-BRAISED MEATBALLS
MAKES 4 SERVINGS

1 pound ground beef

½ cup Italian-seasoned dry bread crumbs

½ cup grated Parmesan cheese

2 eggs, lightly beaten

⅓ cup finely chopped onion

2 cloves garlic, minced

½ teaspoon black pepper

¼ teaspoon salt

1 bottle (12 ounces) craft-brewed lager

1½ cups tomato sauce

1 cup ketchup

½ cup packed brown sugar

2 tablespoons tomato paste

1. Preheat oven to 400°F. Line broiler pan with foil; spray with nonstick cooking spray. Combine beef, bread crumbs, cheese, eggs, onion, garlic, pepper and salt in large bowl; shape mixture into 1-inch balls.

2. Place meatballs on prepared pan. Bake 10 minutes or until browned.

3. Bring beer, tomato sauce, ketchup, brown sugar and tomato paste to a boil in large saucepan or Dutch oven over medium-high heat. Add meatballs; reduce heat to medium-low. Cover; simmer 20 to 30 minutes or until meatballs are cooked through, stirring occasionally.

SMOKY BARBECUED BEEF SANDWICHES
MAKES 6 SERVINGS

  2 onions, thinly sliced and separated into rings
  1 beef brisket (about 3 pounds), trimmed
  ½ teaspoon salt
  ¾ cup craft-brewed blonde ale
  ½ cup packed brown sugar
  ½ cup ketchup
  1½ tablespoons Worcestershire sauce
  1½ tablespoons soy sauce
  2 whole canned chipotle peppers in adobo sauce, finely chopped, plus 1 teaspoon adobo sauce*
  2 cloves garlic, minced
  6 hoagie or Kaiser rolls, split and toasted

For spicier flavor, add 1 to 2 teaspoons additional sauce.

1. Preheat oven to 325°F. Place onions in large roasting pan.

2. Place brisket, fat side up, on top of onions; sprinkle with salt. Combine beer, brown sugar, ketchup, Worcestershire sauce, soy sauce, chipotle peppers, adobo sauce and garlic in medium bowl; pour over brisket. Cover with heavy-duty foil or roasting pan lid. Roast 3 to 3½ hours or until brisket is fork-tender.

3. Transfer brisket to cutting board; tent with foil. Let stand 10 minutes. (Brisket and sauce may be prepared ahead to this point; cool and cover separately. Refrigerate up to 1 day before reheating and serving.)

4. Skim fat from pan juices with large spoon. Transfer juices and onions to large saucepan. Cook over medium heat until thickened, stirring frequently.

5. Trim fat from brisket; carve brisket against the grain into thin slices. Return slices to sauce; mix well. Cook until heated through. Serve slices, onions and sauce in rolls.

POT ROAST CARBONNADE
MAKES 8 SERVINGS

6 thick slices applewood-smoked or other smoked bacon (about 6 ounces)

2 tablespoons all-purpose flour

¾ teaspoon salt

½ teaspoon black pepper

1 beef chuck arm pot roast or chuck shoulder pot roast (about 3½ pounds)

3 large Spanish onions (about 2 pounds), thinly sliced

2 tablespoons brown sugar

1 can (about 14 ounces) beef broth

1 bottle (12 ounces) craft-brewed pilsner

2 teaspoons dried thyme

2 bay leaves

Boiled potatoes or hot cooked egg noodles (optional)

Chopped fresh thyme (optional)

1. Preheat oven to 350°F. Cook bacon in large saucepan or Dutch oven over medium heat until crisp, stirring occasionally. Drain bacon on paper towel-lined plate, reserving drippings in saucepan. Crumble bacon; set aside.

2. Combine flour, salt and pepper in small bowl; spread on sheet of waxed paper. Place pot roast on flour mixture; roll to coat well. Brown pot roast in drippings in saucepan over medium-low heat about 4 to 5 minutes per side. Remove to platter.

3. Pour off all but 2 tablespoons drippings from saucepan. Add onions; cover and cook 10 minutes over medium heat, stirring once. Uncover; sprinkle with brown sugar. Cook, uncovered, over medium-high heat 10 minutes or until onions are golden brown and tender, stirring frequently.

4. Add broth, beer, dried thyme and bay leaves to saucepan; bring to a boil. Return pot roast with any accumulated juices to saucepan. Remove from heat; spoon sauce over top. Cover and bake about 2 hours or until meat is fork-tender.

5. Transfer meat to cutting board; tent with foil.

6. Remove and discard bay leaves. Skim fat from pan juices with large spoon. Place half of juices in food processor; process until smooth. Repeat with remaining juices; return mixture to saucepan. Stir in reserved bacon; cook over medium heat until heated through.

7. Discard bone from roast; carve roast into ¼-inch-thick slices with carving knife. Spoon sauce over roast. Serve with boiled potatoes or hot cooked egg noodles, if desired. Garnish with fresh thyme.

CHEDDAR-BEER BURGERS WITH BACON
MAKES 4 SERVINGS

1½ pounds lean ground beef

4 ounces sharp Cheddar cheese, cut into ½-inch cubes

½ cup craft-brewed blonde ale

¼ cup chopped fresh parsley

1 teaspoon paprika

¾ teaspoon salt

¾ teaspoon garlic powder

¼ teaspoon black pepper

¼ cup ketchup

2 tablespoons mayonnaise

4 hamburger buns

4 lettuce leaves

4 slices tomato

4 thick slices red onion

8 slices bacon, cooked

1. Prepare grill for direct cooking.

2. Combine beef, cheese, beer, parsley, paprika, salt, garlic powder and pepper in large bowl. Mix gently to combine. Shape into four patties, making centers of patties slightly thinner than edges.

3. Grill patties, covered, over medium-high heat 8 to 10 minutes (or uncovered 13 to 15 minutes) for medium (160°F) or to desired doneness, turning once.

4. Meanwhile, combine ketchup and mayonnaise in small bowl. Serve burgers on buns with lettuce, tomato, onion, bacon and ketchup mixture.

BEEF POT PIE
MAKES 4 TO 6 SERVINGS

½ cup all-purpose flour

1 teaspoon salt, divided

½ teaspoon black pepper, divided

1½ pounds lean beef stew meat

2 tablespoons olive oil

1 pound new red potatoes, cubed

2 cups baby carrots

1 cup frozen pearl onions, thawed

1 parsnip, peeled and cut into 1-inch pieces

1 cup craft-brewed stout

¾ cup beef broth

1 teaspoon chopped fresh thyme *or* ½ teaspoon dried thyme

1 refrigerated pie crust (half of 15-ounce package)

1. Preheat oven to 350°F. Combine flour, ½ teaspoon salt and ¼ teaspoon pepper in large resealable food storage bag. Add beef; toss to coat.

2. Heat oil in large skillet over medium-high heat. Add beef and brown on both sides, turning once. Do not crowd meat. Transfer to 2½- to 3-quart casserole. Add potatoes, carrots, onions and parsnip; mix well.

3. Add stout, broth, thyme, remaining ½ teaspoon salt and ¼ teaspoon pepper to same skillet. Bring to a boil, scraping up browned bits from bottom of skillet. Pour into casserole.

4. Cover; bake 2½ to 3 hours or until meat is fork-tender, stirring once. Let stand, uncovered, at room temperature 15 minutes.

5. *Increase oven temperature to 425°F.* Place pie crust over casserole and press edges to seal. Cut slits in crust to vent. Bake 15 to 20 minutes or until crust is golden brown. Cool slightly before serving.

INDIVIDUAL BEEF POT PIES:
Substitute puff pastry for pie crust. Divide beef filling into ovenproof individual serving dishes. Cut puff pastry to fit; press over moistened edges and crimp to seal. Brush tops with 1 egg yolk, lightly beaten. Bake at 400°F for 15 to 20 minutes or until crust is puffed and golden.

VEAL POT ROAST
MAKES 4 TO 6 SERVINGS

2 tablespoons olive oil

1 veal shoulder roast (2½ pounds)

½ teaspoon salt

¼ teaspoon black pepper

¾ pound pearl onions, peeled (see Tip)

½ cup sliced fennel

1 package (3½ ounces) shiitake mushrooms, sliced

6 plum tomatoes, quartered

2 cups chicken broth

1 cup craft-brewed wheat beer

2 cloves garlic, sliced

1 teaspoon minced fresh herbs (rosemary leaves, thyme and/or sage)

¼ teaspoon red pepper flakes

¼ teaspoon grated lemon peel

Hot cooked rice (optional)

SLOW COOKER DIRECTIONS

1. Season roast with salt and black pepper. Heat oil in large skillet over medium-high heat; add roast and brown on all sides. Transfer to slow cooker.

2. Add onions, fennel, mushrooms and tomatoes to slow cooker. Pour broth and beer over roast. Sprinkle with garlic, herbs, red pepper flakes and lemon peel.

3. Cover; cook on LOW 8 to 10 hours or until tender. Remove roast from slow cooker; let rest 10 minutes. Slice roast. Serve with vegetables, sauce and rice, if desired.

★ Tip ★

To peel pearl onions, place in a large pot of boiling water and cook
1 minute. Drain well and run under cold water to cool slightly.
Rub lightly, if necessary. The skins should come off easily.

NOT YOUR MOMMA'S MEAT LOAF
MAKES 6 SERVINGS

2 pounds ground beef, pork and veal meat loaf mix

⅔ cup plain dry bread crumbs

½ cup finely chopped onion

½ cup craft-brewed pale ale

⅓ cup plus 3 tablespoons ketchup, divided

2 eggs

1 tablespoon Dijon mustard

2 teaspoons dried basil

1 teaspoon garlic powder

1 teaspoon salt

½ teaspoon black pepper

1. Preheat oven to 350°F. Spray jelly-roll pan with nonstick cooking spray.

2. Combine meat loaf mix, bread crumbs, onion, ale, 3 tablespoons ketchup, eggs, mustard, basil, garlic powder, salt and pepper in large bowl; mix well. Transfer mixture to prepared pan; shape into 10×5×2-inch loaf. Spread remaining ⅓ cup ketchup over top.

3. Bake 60 to 65 minutes or until cooked through (160°F). Let stand 10 minutes before slicing.

BLACK PEPPER FLANK STEAK WITH BALSAMIC-BEER REDUCTION

MAKES 6 SERVINGS

  1 cup craft-brewed Belgian-style pale ale, divided
  ¼ cup plus 3 tablespoons balsamic vinegar, divided
  4 tablespoons molasses, divided
  3 cloves garlic, minced
  1 flank steak (about 2 pounds)
  ½ cup finely chopped shallots
  ¾ cup beef broth
  3 tablespoons butter
  1¼ teaspoons salt, divided
  1¼ teaspoons black pepper, divided

1. Combine ¾ cup beer, 3 tablespoons vinegar, 2 tablespoons molasses and garlic in large bowl. Add flank steak; turn to coat. Cover and marinate in refrigerator 2 hours or up to 6 hours, turning occasionally.

2. For balsamic-beer reduction, combine shallots, remaining ¼ cup vinegar and ¼ cup beer in small saucepan. Bring to a boil over medium-high heat. Cook 5 to 6 minutes or until almost evaporated and mixture looks like wet sand, stirring occasionally. Add broth and remaining 2 tablespoons molasses; return to a boil. Cook 4 to 5 minutes or until reduced by one third. Remove from heat; stir in butter until melted. Add ¼ teaspoon salt and ¼ teaspoon black pepper.

3. Preheat broiler. Lightly oil broiler rack.

4. Remove steak from marinade and sprinkle both sides with remaining 1 teaspoon salt and 1 teaspoon pepper. Broil 4 inches from heat source 5 to 6 minutes per side for medium-rare (145°F) or to desired doneness. Transfer steak to cutting board; tent with foil. Let stand 10 minutes. Thinly slice and drizzle with balsamic-beer reduction.

PASTRAMI REUBEN SANDWICHES WITH BEER KRAUT

MAKES 4 SERVINGS

1 tablespoon canola oil

½ cup thinly sliced Vidalia or other sweet onion

1 cup well-drained sauerkraut

1 teaspoon sugar

½ cup craft-brewed amber ale

Softened butter

8 slices rye bread

½ cup Russian dressing

4 slices Swiss cheese

1 pound thinly sliced pastrami

1. Heat oil in medium nonstick skillet over medium-high heat. Add onion; cook and stir 2 minutes or until slightly softened. Add sauerkraut and sugar; cook 3 minutes. Pour in beer; cook 3 minutes or until evaporated, stirring occasionally. Remove from heat.

2. Butter one side of each bread slice. Place four slices of bread, butter side down, on work surface. Spread with 1 tablespoon Russian dressing. Top with one fourth of sauerkraut mixture, one slice of Swiss cheese and one fourth of pastrami. Spread unbuttered sides of remaining four slices of bread with remaining Russian dressing; place butter side up on pastrami.

3. Heat large nonstick skillet over medium heat. Place two sandwiches in skillet; press firmly with spatula. Cook 3 minutes or until bread is golden. Turn; place second large skillet on top of sandwiches and press firmly. Cook 4 minutes or until golden. Repeat with remaining two sandwiches.

BEER-BRAISED BRISKET
MAKES 4 TO 6 SERVINGS

3 slices thick-cut bacon, diced

1 beef brisket (about 3 pounds)

2 large onions, thinly sliced

1 bottle (12 ounces) craft-brewed porter

3 cups beef broth

2 tablespoons chopped fresh parsley

1. Preheat oven to 325°F. Cook bacon in large saucepan or Dutch oven over medium heat until crisp, stirring occasionally. Drain bacon on paper towel-lined plate, reserving drippings in saucepan. Brown brisket on both sides in saucepan. Remove to platter.

2. Pour off all but 2 tablespoons drippings from saucepan. Add onions; cook and stir over medium-heat heat 3 to 4 minutes or until softened.

3. Add beer to saucepan. Bring to a boil over medium-high heat, stirring frequently and scraping up any browned bits from bottom of pan. Add brisket and broth; bring to a boil. Cover and cook 3½ to 4 hours or until meat is fork-tender.

4. Remove brisket to cutting board; let rest 10 minutes. Trim off excess fat. Remove onions to platter using slotted spoon. Boil remaining liquid over high heat until slightly thickened.

5. Slice brisket. Top with onions and drizzle with sauce. Sprinkle with bacon and chopped parsley.

GRILLED SKIRT STEAK FAJITAS
MAKES 4 SERVINGS

1½ pounds skirt steak

½ cup craft-brewed pale ale

3 tablespoons lime juice

1 teaspoon ground cumin

2 tablespoons olive oil

1 cup thinly sliced red onion

1 cup thinly sliced red and green bell peppers

2 cloves garlic, minced

3 plum tomatoes, each cut into 4 wedges

1 tablespoon soy sauce

¾ teaspoon salt

¼ teaspoon black pepper

8 (7-inch) flour tortillas

Lime wedges (optional)

1. Place steak in large resealable food storage bag. Combine ale, lime juice and cumin in small bowl; pour over steak. Seal bag; turn to coat. Marinate in refrigerator 2 hours, turning occasionally.

2. Heat oil in large nonstick skillet over medium-high heat. Add onion; cook and stir 2 to 3 minutes or until slightly softened. Add bell peppers; cook and stir 7 to 8 minutes or until softened. Add garlic; cook and stir 1 minute. Add tomatoes; cook 2 minutes or until slightly softened. Add soy sauce; cook 1 minute. Keep warm.

3. Lightly oil grid. Prepare grill for direct cooking.

4. Remove steak from marinade; discard marinade. Sprinkle with salt and black pepper. Grill over medium-high heat 4 to 6 minutes on each side for medium-rare (145°F) or to desired doneness. Transfer to cutting board; cut against grain into ¼-inch slices.

5. Warm tortillas; fill with steak and vegetable mixture. Serve with lime wedges, if desired.

BEEF AND BEER SLIDERS
MAKES 12 SLIDERS

       6 tablespoons ketchup
       2 tablespoons mayonnaise
       2 teaspoons Dijon mustard
1½ pounds ground beef
       ½ cup craft-brewed pilsner
       1 teaspoon salt
       ½ teaspoon garlic powder
       ½ teaspoon onion powder
       ½ teaspoon ground cumin
       ½ teaspoon dried oregano
       ¼ teaspoon black pepper
       3 slices sharp Cheddar cheese, cut into quarters
12 slider or potato dinner rolls
12 baby lettuce leaves
12 plum tomato slices

1. Combine ketchup, mayonnaise and mustard in small bowl; set aside.

2. Combine beef, beer, salt, garlic powder, onion powder, cumin, oregano and pepper in medium bowl. Shape mixture into 12 (¼-inch-thick) patties.

3. Lightly oil grill pan; heat over medium-high heat. Add half of patties; cook 2 minutes. Turn; top each with one piece of cheese. Cook until cheese is melted and patties are cooked through. Transfer to plate and keep warm. Repeat with remaining patties and cheese.

4. Serves sliders on rolls with lettuce leaves and tomato slices.

ON THE GRILL

BEER-BRINED GRILLED PORK CHOPS
MAKES 4 SERVINGS

1 bottle (12 ounces) craft-brewed porter or other dark beer

¼ cup packed dark brown sugar

1 tablespoon salt

1 tablespoon chili powder

2 cloves garlic, minced

3 cups ice water

4 pork chops (1 inch thick)

Grilled Rosemary Potatoes (recipe follows)

1. Whisk beer, brown sugar, salt, chili powder and garlic in medium bowl until salt is dissolved. Add ice water; stir until ice melts. Add pork chops; place plate on top to keep chops submerged in brine. Marinate in refrigerator 3 to 4 hours.

2. Prepare grill for direct cooking. Prepare Grilled Rosemary Potatoes; place packet on grid. Drain pork chops and pat dry with paper towels. Grill pork chops, covered, over medium heat 10 to 12 minutes or until cooked through (145°F). Serve immediately.

TIP:
Brining adds flavor and moisture to meats. Be sure to buy pork chops that have not been injected with a sodium solution or they could end up too salty.

GRILLED ROSEMARY POTATOES:
Place 4 quartered red potatoes, ¼ cup sliced onion, ¼ cup sliced red bell pepper, 2 teaspoons chopped fresh rosemary and 1 teaspoon red pepper flakes on a 13×9-inch piece of heavy-duty foil. Toss mixture on foil; top with an additional 13×9-inch piece of foil. Fold edges to make a packet. Grill 12 to 15 minutes or until potatoes are tender.

ORANGE-MARINATED TUNA STEAKS WITH NECTARINE SALSA

MAKES 4 SERVINGS

NECTARINE SALSA

2 large nectarines, pitted and diced

3 tablespoons finely chopped red onion

½ jalapeño pepper, seeded and minced

2 tablespoons chopped fresh cilantro

1 tablespoon lime juice

¼ teaspoon salt

TUNA

½ cup craft-brewed pilsner

⅓ cup chopped green onions

¼ cup orange juice

¼ cup soy sauce

2 tablespoons sugar

2 tablespoons lemon juice

2 tablespoons grated fresh ginger

2 cloves garlic, minced

4 (6- to 8-ounce) tuna steaks, about ¾ inch thick

1. For salsa, combine nectarines, onion, jalapeño pepper, cilantro, lime juice and salt in medium bowl. Cover and refrigerate.

2. For tuna, combine beer, green onions, orange juice, soy sauce, sugar, lemon juice, ginger and garlic in large bowl; mix well. Add tuna; turn to coat. Marinate in refrigerator 30 minutes, turning occasionally.

3. Lightly oil grid. Prepare grill for direct cooking.

4. Grill tuna over medium-high heat 3 minutes per side or until nicely marked and pink in center. Serve with salsa.

GRILLED CHICKEN BREAST SANDWICHES WITH BEER-BRAISED ONIONS

MAKES 4 SERVINGS

4 boneless skinless chicken breasts (4 ounces each), pounded slightly

½ cup craft-brewed lager

3 tablespoons Dijon mustard

1 tablespoon paprika

1 tablespoon olive oil

2 cloves garlic, minced

1 teaspoon dried basil

Beer-Braised Onions (recipe follows)

¾ teaspoon salt

¼ teaspoon black pepper

4 English muffins, toasted

4 lettuce leaves (optional)

4 tomato slices (optional)

1. Combine chicken, lager, mustard, paprika, oil, garlic and basil in large resealable food storage bag. Seal bag; turn to coat. Marinate in refrigerator 2 hours, turning occasionally.

2. Lightly oil grid. Prepare grill for direct cooking. Prepare Beer-Braised Onions.

3. Remove chicken from bag; discard marinade. Sprinkle chicken with salt and pepper. Grill, covered, 4 to 6 minutes on each side or until cooked through (165°F).

4. Serve chicken and onions on English muffins with lettuce and tomato, if desired.

BEER-BRAISED ONIONS:
Melt 1 tablespoon butter in medium saucepan over medium-high heat. Add 1½ cups thinly sliced red onions (about 1 medium onion) and 2 tablespoons sugar; cook 5 to 7 minutes or until onion is soft but not browned, stirring occasionally. Stir in 2 tablespoons craft-brewed lager, 1 tablespoon balsamic vinegar and ½ teaspoon salt; cook 1 minute or until liquid evaporates.

PARMESAN HONEY LAGER BURGERS
MAKES 4 SERVINGS

¾ cup craft-brewed honey lager, divided

3 tablespoons mayonnaise

3 tablespoons ketchup

½ teaspoon yellow mustard

1½ pounds ground beef

⅓ cup grated Parmesan cheese

1 tablespoon Worcestershire sauce

¼ teaspoon black pepper

4 hamburger buns

8 tomato slices

8 thin red onion slices

1. Lightly oil grid. Prepare grill for direct cooking. Combine 1 tablespoon lager, mayonnaise, ketchup and mustard in small bowl; set aside.

2. Combine beef, ¼ cup lager, cheese, Worcestershire sauce and pepper in large bowl; mix lightly. Shape into four patties, making centers of patties slightly thinner than edges.

3. Grill burgers over medium-high heat 6 to 8 minutes for medium-rare (145°F) or to desired doneness, turning once and basting often with remaining lager.

4. Serve burgers on buns with tomatoes, onions and mayonnaise mixture.

GRILLED SALMON WITH PINEAPPLE SALSA

MAKES 4 SERVINGS

½ pineapple, cut into ½-inch cubes (about 2 cups)

½ cup craft-brewed Vienna-style lager or light-colored lager

1 tablespoon sugar

¼ cup finely chopped red onion

¼ cup finely chopped red bell pepper

2 tablespoons chopped fresh cilantro

1 tablespoon lime juice

1 teaspoon salt, divided

4 salmon fillets (6 to 8 ounces each)

1 tablespoon olive oil

¼ teaspoon black pepper

1. Combine pineapple, beer and sugar in medium bowl; refrigerate 1 hour. Drain and discard all but 2 tablespoons liquid. Add onion, bell pepper, cilantro, lime juice and ½ teaspoon salt to pineapple mixture; refrigerate 1 hour or overnight.

2. Lightly oil grid. Prepare grill for direct cooking. Rub salmon fillets with oil and sprinkle with remaining ½ teaspoon salt and black pepper.

3. Grill over medium-high heat 5 minutes per side or until salmon just begins to flake when tested with fork. Serve with salsa.

BEER-BASTED BARBECUE PORK CHOPS

MAKES 6 SERVINGS

1 cup plus 3 tablespoons craft-brewed honey wheat beer, divided

1 cup barbecue sauce, divided

3 tablespoons honey

1 tablespoon chili powder

6 bone-in loin pork chops, 1 inch thick

1 teaspoon salt

½ teaspoon black pepper

1. Combine 1 cup beer, ½ cup barbecue sauce, honey and chili powder in large bowl; mix well. Add pork chops; turn to coat. Marinate in refrigerator 2 hours or up to 4 hours, turning occasionally.

2. Combine remaining ½ cup barbecue sauce and 3 tablespoons beer in separate bowl; set aside.

3. Lightly oil grid. Prepare grill for direct cooking.

4. Remove pork chops from marinade and sprinkle with salt and black pepper. Grill pork chops 11 to 12 minutes or until cooked through (145°F), turning several times and basting with reserved barbecue sauce mixture.

GUADALAJARA BEEF

MAKES 4 SERVINGS

1 bottle (12 ounces) craft-brewed Vienna-style lager

¼ cup soy sauce

3 cloves garlic, minced

1 teaspoon ground cumin

1 teaspoon chili powder

½ teaspoon ground red pepper

1 beef flank steak (about 1 pound)

6 medium yellow, red and green bell peppers, cut lengthwise into quarters

8 (6- to 8-inch) flour tortillas

Lime wedges

Salsa (optional)

1. Combine beer, soy sauce, garlic, cumin, chili powder and ground red pepper in large resealable food storage bag; add beef. Seal bag; turn to coat. Marinate in refrigerator up to 24 hours, turning occasionally.

2. Prepare grill for direct cooking.

3. Remove beef from marinade; discard marinade. Grill beef, uncovered, over medium heat 17 to 21 minutes for medium-rare (145°F) or to desired doneness, turning once. Meanwhile, grill bell peppers 7 to 10 minutes or until tender, turning once.

4. Cut steak against grain into thin slices and thickly slice bell peppers. Serve on tortillas with lime wedges and salsa, if desired.

CHIPOTLE STRIP STEAKS
MAKES 4 SERVINGS

   1 tablespoon olive oil

   ⅓ cup finely chopped onion

   ¾ cup craft-brewed lager

   1 teaspoon Worcestershire sauce

   ⅓ cup ketchup

   1 tablespoon red wine vinegar

   1 teaspoon sugar

   ⅛ to ¼ teaspoon chipotle chili powder

   4 bone-in strip steaks (8 to 9 ounces each)

   1 teaspoon salt

1. Heat oil in small saucepan over medium-high heat. Add onion; cook and stir 5 minutes or until softened. Pour in beer and Worcestershire sauce; bring to a boil, stirring occasionally. Continue cooking until mixture is reduced to about ⅓ cup. Stir in ketchup, vinegar, sugar and chili powder. Reduce heat to medium-low; simmer 3 minutes or until thickened, stirring occasionally. Keep warm.

2. Lightly oil grid. Prepare grill for direct cooking.

3. Sprinkle steaks with salt. Grill steaks over medium-high heat 4 to 5 minutes on each side for medium-rare (145°F) or to desired doneness. Serve steaks with chipotle sauce.

GRILLED PIZZA MARGHERITA
MAKES 4 SERVINGS

¾ cup craft-brewed pilsner or lager

1 package (¼ ounce) active dry yeast

2 tablespoons plus 2 teaspoons extra virgin olive oil, divided

1¾ to 2½ cups all-purpose flour

1 teaspoon salt

1½ pints grape tomatoes, halved

1 clove garlic, minced

¼ teaspoon dried basil

⅛ teaspoon salt

⅛ teaspoon red pepper flakes

6 ounces fresh mozzarella, cut into 12 slices

10 fresh basil leaves, thinly sliced

1. Microwave beer in small microwavable bowl on HIGH 25 seconds. Stir in yeast and 2 teaspoons oil; let stand 5 minutes or until foamy. Combine 1¾ cups flour and salt in medium bowl. Add beer mixture; stir until dough pulls away from side of bowl, adding additional flour as needed. Turn dough out onto floured surface. Knead 6 to 7 minutes, adding enough additional flour to make smooth and elastic dough.

2. Divide dough in half. Shape into two balls. Dust with flour; place in separate medium bowls. Cover with plastic wrap; let rise in warm place about 1½ hours or until doubled in size.

3. Heat 1 tablespoon oil in medium nonstick skillet over medium-high heat. Add tomatoes, garlic, basil, salt and red pepper flakes; cook 3 to 4 minutes or until tomatoes are very soft, stirring occasionally. Set aside.

4. Lightly oil grid. Prepare grill for direct cooking over high heat.

5. Working with one ball at a time, turn dough out onto lightly floured surface. Roll out each into 9-inch round. Transfer to floured baking sheets. Brush tops of each round with half of remaining 2 teaspoons oil. Cover; let stand 10 minutes.

6. *Reduce grill to medium heat.* Carefully flip dough rounds onto grid, oiled side down. Grill, uncovered, 3 minutes or until bottoms are golden and well marked. Turn crusts; spread with tomato mixture, leaving ½-inch border. Top with cheese; grill, covered, 3 minutes or until cheese begins to melt and crusts are golden brown. Transfer to cutting board; sprinkle with basil.

HOISIN CHICKEN THIGHS
MAKES 4 SERVINGS

¾ cup hoisin sauce

¾ cup craft-brewed Japanese-style rice lager

3 tablespoons grated fresh ginger

5 cloves garlic, minced

3 tablespoons packed dark brown sugar

3 tablespoons soy sauce

8 chicken thighs (about 2½ pounds)

1. Combine hoisin sauce, beer, ginger, garlic, brown sugar and soy sauce in large bowl. Reserve ½ cup mixture; refrigerate until needed. Add chicken thighs to remaining marinade in bowl; turn to coat. Refrigerate 2 hours or overnight, turning occasionally.

2. Lightly oil grid. Prepare grill for indirect cooking.

3. Grill chicken, skin side down, covered, over medium-high heat 40 minutes or until 170°F, turning occasionally and basting with reserved hoisin mixture after first 20 minutes. Do not baste during last 5 minutes of cooking.

HONEY-MUSTARD AND
BEER PULLED PORK SANDWICHES

MAKES 8 SERVINGS

  1 tablespoon chili powder

  2 teaspoons ground cumin

½ teaspoon salt

  2 tablespoons yellow mustard

  1 bone-in pork shoulder roast (about 2 pounds)

  2 bottles (12 ounces each) craft-brewed honey beer, divided

¾ cup ketchup

  3 tablespoons honey

  2 tablespoons cider vinegar

  8 soft sandwich rolls

24 bread and butter pickle chips

1. Prepare grill for indirect cooking over medium-low heat.

2. Combine chili powder, cumin and salt in small bowl. Spread mustard on all sides of pork; cover evenly with cumin mixture. Transfer pork to rack in disposable foil pan. Reserve ¾ cup beer. Pour enough remaining beer into foil pan to just cover rack beneath pork. Place on grid opposite heat source. Grill, covered, 4 to 6 hours or until internal temperature reaches 160°F. Transfer to cutting board; tent with foil. Let stand 15 minutes.

3. Combine reserved ¾ cup beer, ketchup, honey and vinegar in small saucepan. Bring to a boil over medium-high heat. Reduce heat to medium; cook and stir until thickened.

4. Shred pork with two forks, discarding bone and fat. Combine pork and sauce in medium bowl; toss gently to combine. Serve on rolls with pickles.

CHIPOTLE SPICE-RUBBED BEER CAN CHICKEN
MAKES 4 SERVINGS

2 tablespoons packed brown sugar

2 teaspoons smoked paprika

2 teaspoons ground cumin

1 teaspoon salt

1 teaspoon garlic powder

1 teaspoon chili powder

½ teaspoon chipotle chili powder

1 whole chicken (3½ to 4 pounds), rinsed and patted dry

1 can (12 ounces) craft-brewed pilsner

1. Lightly oil grid. Prepare grill for indirect cooking.

2. Combine brown sugar, paprika, cumin, salt, garlic powder, chili powder and chipotle chili powder in small bowl. Gently loosen skin of chicken over breast, legs and thighs. Rub sugar mixture under and over skin and inside cavity. Pour out one fourth of beer. Hold chicken upright with cavity pointing down; insert beer can into cavity.

3. Stand chicken and can upright on grid opposite heat source over drip pan. Spread legs slightly to help support chicken. Grill, covered, over medium heat 1 hour 15 minutes or until chicken is tender and cooked through (165°F).

4. Lift chicken off grid using metal tongs. Let rest upright on cutting board 5 minutes. Carefully remove and discard beer can. Carve chicken.

SPICE-RUBBED BEEF BRISKET
MAKES 12 SERVINGS

2 cups hickory chips

1 teaspoon salt

1 teaspoon paprika

1 teaspoon chili powder

1 teaspoon garlic pepper

1 beef brisket (3 to 3½ pounds)

¼ cup craft-brewed amber ale

1 tablespoon Worcestershire sauce

1 tablespoon balsamic vinegar

1 teaspoon olive oil

¼ teaspoon dry mustard

6 ears corn, cut into 2-inch pieces

12 small new potatoes

6 carrots, cut into 2-inch pieces

2 green bell peppers, cut into 2-inch squares

6 tablespoons lemon juice

6 tablespoons water

1½ teaspoons dried Italian seasoning

1. Soak hickory chips in water 30 minutes. Prepare grill for indirect cooking. Bank briquets on either side of water-filled drip pan.

2. Combine salt, paprika, chili powder and garlic pepper in small bowl. Rub spice mixture onto both sides of brisket. Loosely cover with foil; set aside. Combine beer, Worcestershire sauce, vinegar, oil and dry mustard in small bowl; set aside.

3. Drain hickory chips; sprinkle ½ cup over coals. Place brisket on grid directly over drip pan. Grill, covered, over medium heat 30 minutes. Baste with reserved beer mixture. Continue grilling 3 hours or until meat thermometer reaches 160°F when inserted into thickest part of brisket, turning over every 30 minutes. (Add 4 to 9 briquets and ¼ cup hickory chips to each side of fire every hour.)

4. Alternately thread corn, potatoes, carrots and bell peppers onto metal skewers. Combine lemon juice, water and Italian seasoning in small bowl; brush onto vegetables. Grill 20 to 25 minutes or until tender, turning once.

5. Remove brisket to cutting board; tent loosely with foil. Let stand 10 minutes before carving. Serve with vegetables.

MAPLE AND HONEY WHEAT CHICKEN THIGHS

MAKES 6 SERVINGS

  1 bottle (12 ounces) craft-brewed honey wheat beer, divided

⅔ cup orange juice, divided

¼ cup plus 2 tablespoons maple syrup, divided

  2 tablespoons lemon juice

  2 cloves garlic, minced

  2 teaspoons grated fresh ginger, divided

  6 chicken thighs (2 to 2¼ pounds)

  2 teaspoons water

  2 teaspoons cornstarch

1¼ teaspoons salt

¼ teaspoon black pepper

1. Combine ¾ cup beer, ⅓ cup orange juice, 2 tablespoons maple syrup, lemon juice, garlic and 1 teaspoon ginger in large resealable food storage bag. Add chicken. Seal bag; turn to coat. Marinate in refrigerator 2 hours or overnight.

2. Meanwhile, combine remaining ¾ cup beer, ⅓ cup orange juice, ¼ cup maple syrup and 1 teaspoon ginger in small saucepan. Bring to a boil over medium-high heat. Reduce heat to medium; simmer about 4 minutes or until slightly thickened.

3. Stir water into cornstarch in small bowl until smooth. Add cornstarch mixture, salt and pepper to saucepan; increase heat to high and boil 1 minute or until thickened. Remove from heat.

4. Lightly oil grid. Prepare grill for indirect cooking. Remove chicken from marinade; discard marinade. Grill chicken, skin side down, covered, 35 to 38 minutes or until cooked through (165°F), turning occasionally and brushing with glaze. Do not brush with glaze during last 5 minutes of cooking.

CHICKEN AND VEGETABLE SATAY WITH PEANUT SAUCE

MAKES 4 SERVINGS

1½ pounds boneless skinless chicken thighs, cut into 32 (1½-inch) pieces

⅔ cup craft-brewed Japanese-style rice lager, divided

3 tablespoons packed dark brown sugar, divided

1 tablespoon plus 2 teaspoons lime juice, divided

3 cloves garlic, minced, divided

1¼ teaspoons curry powder, divided

½ cup coconut milk

½ cup chunky peanut butter

1 tablespoon fish sauce

3 tablespoons peanut oil, divided

¼ cup finely chopped onion

24 medium mushrooms, stems trimmed

4 green onions, cut into 24 (1-inch) pieces

Hot cooked noodles (optional)

1. Place chicken in large resealable food storage bag. Combine ⅓ cup beer, 1 tablespoon brown sugar, 1 tablespoon lime juice, 2 cloves garlic and 1 teaspoon curry powder in small bowl. Pour over chicken. Seal bag; turn to coat. Marinate in refrigerator 2 hours, turning occasionally.

2. Meanwhile for peanut sauce, combine coconut milk, peanut butter, fish sauce and remaining ⅓ cup beer, 2 tablespoons sugar and 2 teaspoons lime juice in medium bowl. Heat 1 tablespoon oil in small saucepan over medium-high heat. Add onion and remaining clove garlic; cook 2 to 3 minutes or until just starting to soften. Add remaining ¼ teaspoon curry powder; cook 15 seconds. Stir in coconut milk mixture. Reduce heat to medium; simmer about 15 minutes or until thickened, stirring frequently. Keep warm.

3. Lightly oil grid. Prepare grill for direct cooking. Remove chicken from marinade; discard marinade. Alternately thread chicken, mushrooms and green onions onto 8 skewers. Brush skewers with remaining 2 tablespoons oil. Grill 8 to 10 minutes or until chicken is cooked through (165°F) and mushrooms are tender, turning occasionally. Serve with peanut sauce and noodles.

BEER GRILLED STEAKS

MAKES 4 SERVINGS

1 cup craft-beer lager or other light-colored beer
¼ cup soy sauce
2 tablespoons molasses
2 cloves garlic, minced
½ teaspoon salt
¼ teaspoon black pepper
4 rib-eye steaks, 1 inch thick (4 to 6 ounces each)

1. Whisk beer, soy sauce, molasses, garlic, salt and pepper in small bowl. Place steaks in resealable food storage bag. Pour beer mixture over steaks. Seal bag; turn to coat. Marinate in refrigerator at least 2 hours.

2. Prepare grill for direct cooking. Grill steaks, covered, over high heat 8 to 10 minutes per side for medium-rare (145°F) or to desired doneness.

SPICY SMOKED BEEF RIBS

MAKES 4 TO 6 SERVINGS

    4 wood chunks for smoking

    4 to 6 pounds beef back ribs, cut into 3- to 4-rib pieces

    Black pepper

1⅓ cups barbecue sauce

    2 teaspoons hot pepper sauce or Szechuan chili sauce

    2 to 3 bottles (12 ounces each) craft-brewed lager, at room temperature

1. Soak wood chunks in water at least 30 minutes; drain.

2. Spread ribs on baking sheet; season with black pepper. Combine barbecue sauce and hot pepper sauce in small bowl. Brush ribs with half of sauce. Cover; marinate in refrigerator 30 minutes to 1 hour.

3. Prepare grill for indirect cooking. Add soaked wood to fire. Place foil drip pan in center of grill; fill pan half full with beer. Replace grid.

4. Place ribs on grid, meaty side up, directly above drip pan. Grill ribs over low heat, covered, about 1 hour or until meat is tender, brushing remaining sauce over ribs several times during cooking. (If grill has thermometer, maintain cooking temperature between 250°F to 275°F. Add a few more briquets as needed to maintain constant temperature.) Add more soaked wood chunks after 30 minutes, if necessary.

SPECIALS ON TAP

FISH AND CHIPS
MAKES 4 SERVINGS

¾ cup all-purpose flour

½ cup flat craft-brewed pilsner*

1 egg, separated

   Vegetable oil

4 medium russet potatoes, each cut into 8 wedges

   Salt

1 pound cod fillets (about 6 to 8 small fillets)

   Malt vinegar (optional)

   Lemon wedges (optional)

To flatten beer, open at least 1 hour before using.

1. Combine flour, beer and 2 teaspoons oil in small bowl. Cover and refrigerate 1 to 2 hours.

2. Stir egg yolk into flour mixture. Beat egg white in medium bowl with electric mixer at high speed until soft peaks form. Fold egg white into flour mixture.

3. Heat 2 inches of oil in large heavy skillet over medium heat until it reaches 365°F; adjust heat to maintain temperature. Add potato wedges to hot oil in batches. (Do not crowd.) Fry 4 to 6 minutes or until browned, turning once. Remove to wire racks or paper towels to drain; sprinkle lightly with salt.

4. Return oil to 365°F. Dip fish pieces into batter in batches; add to hot oil. Fry 4 to 6 minutes or until batter is crispy and brown and fish begins to flake when tested with fork, turning once. (Allow temperature of oil to return to 365°F between batches.) Remove to wire racks or paper towels to drain. Serve immediately with potato wedges. Sprinkle with vinegar and serve with lemon wedges, if desired.

CERVEZA CHICKEN ENCHILADA CASSEROLE

MAKES 4 TO 6 SERVINGS

    2 cups water
    1 bottle (12 ounces) craft-brewed Vienna-style lager, divided
    1 stalk celery, chopped
    1 small carrot, chopped
      Juice of 1 lime
    1 teaspoon salt
1½ pounds boneless skinless chicken breasts
    1 can (about 10 ounces) enchilada sauce
    1 bag (9 ounces) white corn tortilla chips
  ½ medium onion, chopped
    3 cups (12 ounces) shredded Cheddar cheese
      Sour cream, sliced olives and chopped green onions (optional)

SLOW COOKER DIRECTIONS

1. Combine water, 1 cup beer, celery, carrot, lime juice and salt in large saucepan. Bring to a boil over high heat. Add chicken; reduce heat to medium-low. Cook 12 to 14 minutes or until chicken is cooked through. Cool chicken; shred with two forks.

2. Pour one third of enchilada sauce into slow cooker. Arrange one third of tortilla chips over sauce. Layer with one third of shredded chicken and one third of chopped onion. Sprinkle with 1 cup cheese. Repeat layers two more times, pouring remaining 1 cup beer over casserole before adding last cup of cheese.

3. Cover; cook on LOW 3½ to 4 hours. Garnish with sour cream, sliced olives and green onions.

TANGY BARBECUED LAMB
MAKES 6 SERVINGS

¾ cup chili sauce

½ cup craft-brewed honey beer

½ cup honey

¼ cup finely chopped onion

¼ cup Worcestershire sauce

2 cloves garlic, minced

½ teaspoon red pepper flakes

¼ teaspoon sea salt

5 pounds lamb ribs, well trimmed and cut into individual ribs

1. Combine chili sauce, beer, honey, onion, Worcestershire sauce, garlic, red pepper flakes and salt in small saucepan; bring to a boil over medium-high heat. Reduce heat to medium-low. Simmer, covered, 10 minutes. Remove from heat; cool to room temperature.

2. Place lamb in large resealable food storage bag; add marinade. Seal bag; turn to coat. Marinate in refrigerator at least 2 hours, turning occasionally.

3. Oil grid. Prepare grill for indirect cooking.

4. Remove lamb from marinade; reserve marinade. Arrange lamb on grid over drip pan over medium heat. Grill, covered, 45 minutes or until tender, turning lamb and brushing with marinade twice. Place remaining marinade in small saucepan and bring to a boil over medium-high heat; boil 1 minute. Serve with lamb.

NOTE:
To set up gas grill for indirect cooking, preheat all burners on high. Turn one burner off; place food over "off" burner. Reset remaining burners to medium. To set up charcoal grill for indirect cooking, arrange hot coals around outer edge of grill; place disposable aluminum pan in open space. Place food over pan.

PILSNER PARMESAN POTATOES

MAKES 4 TO 6 SERVINGS

4 pounds Yukon Gold potatoes, thinly sliced

1 cup minced sweet onion

1 bottle (12 ounces) craft-brewed pilsner

1 cup grated Parmesan cheese

½ cup whipping cream

1 tablespoon all-purpose flour

1 teaspoon paprika

½ teaspoon salt

½ teaspoon black pepper

1. Preheat oven to 350°F. Grease 13×9-inch baking dish. Place potatoes in dish. Sprinkle with onion.

2. Combine pilsner, cheese, cream, flour, paprika, salt and pepper in medium bowl. Pour over potato mixture; stir gently to coat potatoes evenly.

3. Cover baking dish with foil; bake 30 minutes. Remove foil; bake 15 minutes or until potatoes are golden brown and sauce is bubbly. Let stand 15 minutes before serving.

BOCK BBQ BEAN SALAD
MAKES 4 TO 6 SERVINGS

⅓ cup spicy barbecue sauce

¼ cup craft-brewed bock

3 tablespoons cider vinegar

1 tablespoon molasses

1 teaspoon hot pepper sauce

½ teaspoon mustard seeds

1 can (about 15 ounces) pinto beans, rinsed and drained

3 plum tomatoes, seeded and coarsely chopped

4 stalks celery, halved lengthwise and sliced

½ cup chopped green onions

Salt and black pepper

Additional hot pepper sauce (optional)

Large lettuce leaves (optional)

1. Combine barbecue sauce, beer, vinegar, molasses, hot pepper sauce and mustard seeds in large bowl.

2. Add beans, tomatoes, celery and green onions; toss to coat. Season with salt, black pepper and additional hot pepper sauce, if desired. Serve in lettuce-lined bowl, if desired.

★ Tip ★

This salad will keep, covered, in refrigerator for up to 2 days.
Bring it to room temperature before serving

GREEK-STYLE BRAISED LAMB CHOPS

MAKES 4 SERVINGS

1 teaspoon dried Greek seasoning

4 lamb shoulder chops (about 2½ pounds)

3 tablespoons olive oil

1 large onion, halved and sliced

1 bottle (12 ounces) craft-brewed pilsner

3 plum tomatoes, each cut into 6 wedges

½ cup pitted kalamata olives

1 tablespoon chopped fresh parsley

1. Rub Greek seasoning on all sides of chops.

2. Heat oil in large saucepan over medium-high heat. Brown chops on all sides in batches. Remove chops to plate. Add onion to saucepan; cook and stir until soft. Increase heat to high; pour in beer. Bring to a boil, stirring to scrape up browned bits. Reduce heat to low; add chops, tomatoes and olives. Cover; simmer over low heat 1 hour or until meat is tender.

3. Remove chops and vegetables to serving platter. Tent with foil. Bring remaining liquid to a boil over high heat; cook until slightly thickened and reduced to about 1 cup. Pour sauce over chops and vegetables; sprinkle with parsley.

SLOW COOKER CHICKEN CURRY
MAKES 4 SERVINGS

⅓ cup vegetable oil

1 whole chicken (3½ to 4 pounds), cut into 8 pieces

1 cup chicken broth

1 cup craft-brewed India pale ale

1 cup tomato sauce

1 large onion, chopped

1 tablespoon minced fresh ginger

2½ teaspoons curry powder

1 teaspoon salt

1 teaspoon garam masala

2 cloves garlic, minced

½ teaspoon chili powder

⅛ teaspoon ground red pepper

4 cups hot cooked basmati rice

SLOW COOKER DIRECTIONS

1. Heat oil in large skillet over medium-high heat. Working in batches, brown chicken on all sides.

2. Place chicken in slow cooker. Add broth, beer, tomato sauce, onion, ginger, curry powder, salt, garam masala, garlic, chili powder and ground red pepper.

3. Cover; cook on LOW 8 hours. Serve chicken with sauce over rice.

POTATO, BEER AND CHEESE GRATIN

MAKES 8 SERVINGS

1 bottle (12 ounces) craft-brewed pale ale

2 sprigs fresh thyme

1 bay leaf

½ cup whipping cream

1 tablespoon all-purpose flour

2 cloves garlic, minced

2 pounds potatoes (about 3 large), thinly sliced

1 teaspoon salt

1 teaspoon black pepper

2 cups (8 ounces) shredded Gruyère or Emmentaler cheese

2 tablespoons chopped fresh chives (optional)

1. Bring beer, thyme and bay leaf to a boil in medium saucepan over medium-high heat. Reduce heat to low. Simmer 5 minutes or until liquid reduces to ¾ cup, stirring occasionally. Remove and discard thyme and bay leaf. Let cool.

2. Combine cream, flour and garlic in small bowl; mix well. Stir into beer.

3. Preheat oven to 375°F. Grease 13×9-inch baking dish. Arrange half of potato slices in bottom of prepared dish, overlapping slightly. Sprinkle with salt and pepper. Pour half of beer mixture over potatoes; sprinkle with half of cheese. Repeat layers.

4. Cover with foil; bake 30 minutes. *Reduce oven temperature to 350°F.* Uncover; bake 30 minutes or until potatoes are tender and top is golden brown. Let stand 10 minutes before serving. Garnish with chives.

VARIATION:

Add 1 teaspoon of minced jalapeño peppers to the gratin for extra spice and a taste that balances well with beer. Add the jalapeños with the cheese in step 3.

BACON-WRAPPED SCALLOPS

MAKES 12 SERVINGS

24 sea scallops, side muscle removed

½ cup craft-brewed Belgian-style wit (white ale)

3 tablespoons chopped fresh cilantro

2 tablespoons honey

¼ teaspoon ground chipotle pepper

12 slices bacon, halved

1. Combine scallops, ale, cilantro, honey and chipotle pepper in medium bowl; stir to coat. Cover and refrigerate 30 minutes.

2. Preheat broiler. Lightly oil baking sheet.

3. Place 1 scallop on 1 bacon half. Wrap bacon around scallop and secure with toothpick. Transfer to prepared baking sheet. Repeat with remaining bacon and scallops. Brush with marinade.

4. Broil 5 inches from heat 4 minutes. Turn; broil 3 minutes or until scallops are cooked through. Serve hot or at room temperature.

SLOW COOKER BEER BOLOGNESE
MAKES 6 TO 8 SERVINGS

3 slices bacon, chopped

1 large onion, chopped

1 stalk celery, chopped

1 carrot, chopped

2 cloves garlic, minced

3 teaspoons olive oil, divided

8 ounces mushrooms, sliced

¾ pound ground beef

¾ pound ground pork

1 can (28 ounces) tomato purée

1 bottle (12 ounces) craft-brewed porter

1 cup beef broth

1 tablespoon tomato paste

1 teaspoon salt

¼ teaspoon black pepper

¼ teaspoon red pepper flakes

Hot cooked pasta

Shaved Parmesan cheese and chopped fresh parsley

SLOW COOKER DIRECTIONS

1. Cook bacon in large skillet over medium-high heat until crisp. Remove bacon to paper towel-lined plate with slotted spoon, reserving drippings.

2. Add onion, celery and carrot to same skillet; cook and stir 5 minutes or until beginning to brown. Add garlic; cook and stir 1 minute. Transfer vegetables to slow cooker. Add 1 teaspoon oil to skillet. Add mushrooms; cook and stir until beginning to brown. Transfer to slow cooker.

3. Heat remaining 2 teaspoons oil in skillet. Brown beef and pork over medium-high heat, stirring to break up meat. Drain fat. Transfer meat to slow cooker. Add bacon, tomato purée, beer, broth, tomato paste, salt, black pepper and red pepper flakes to slow cooker. Cover; cook on LOW 8 to 10 hours. Serve over pasta; top with Parmesan and parsley.

BEER-BRINED CHICKEN

MAKES 4 SERVINGS

4 cups water

3 cups craft-brewed stout or porter

2 cups apple juice

½ cup plus ½ teaspoon kosher salt, divided

½ cup packed brown sugar

1 teaspoon paprika

1 sprig fresh rosemary

1 bay leaf

1 whole chicken (3½ to 4 pounds)

¼ cup (½ stick) butter, melted

1 tablespoon chopped fresh rosemary

¼ teaspoon black pepper

1. Combine water, stout, apple juice, ½ cup salt, brown sugar, paprika, rosemary sprig and bay leaf in large saucepan or Dutch oven. Stir until salt and sugar are dissolved. Add chicken; cover and refrigerate 2 to 4 hours.

2. Preheat oven to 425°F. Remove chicken from brine; pat dry. Tie drumsticks together to maintain best shape. Place on rack in roasting pan. Cover loosely with foil; roast 45 minutes.

3. Remove foil. Combine butter, chopped rosemary, remaining ½ teaspoon salt and pepper in small bowl; brush over chicken. Continue roasting until cooked through (165°F). If chicken begins to get too dark, cover loosely with foil.

4. Let stand 10 minutes before carving.

CHEDDAR AND LEEK STRATA
MAKES 12 SERVINGS

8 eggs, lightly beaten

2 cups milk

½ cup craft-brewed porter or stout

2 cloves garlic, minced

¼ teaspoon salt

¼ teaspoon black pepper

1 loaf (16 ounces) sourdough bread, cut into ½-inch cubes

2 small leeks, coarsely chopped

1 red bell pepper, chopped

1½ cups (6 ounces) shredded Swiss cheese

1½ cups (6 ounces) shredded sharp Cheddar cheese

1. Grease 13×9-inch baking dish. Beat eggs, milk, porter, garlic, salt and black pepper in large bowl until well blended.

2. Spread half of bread cubes in bottom of prepared dish. Sprinkle half of leeks and half of bell pepper over bread cubes. Top with ¾ cup Swiss cheese and ¾ cup Cheddar cheese. Repeat layers. Pour egg mixture evenly over top.

3. Cover tightly with plastic wrap or foil. Weigh top down with slightly smaller baking dish. Refrigerate at least 2 hours or overnight.

4. Preheat oven to 350°F. Bake, uncovered, 40 to 45 minutes or until center is set. Serve immediately.

PORK LOIN WITH APPLE, ONION AND BEER MARMALADE

MAKES 8 SERVINGS

1 bone-in pork loin (about 4 pounds)
½ teaspoon salt
¼ teaspoon black pepper
⅛ teaspoon ground cinnamon
    Apple, Onion and Beer Marmalade (recipe follows)

1. Preheat oven to 450°F. Place pork in large roasting pan; sprinkle with salt, pepper and cinnamon.

2. Roast pork 15 minutes. *Reduce oven temperature to 300°F.* Roast 1 hour 15 minutes or until 155°F. Tent loosely with foil; let rest 5 minutes before slicing.

3. Meanwhile, prepare Apple, Onion and Beer Marmalade. Serve over sliced pork.

APPLE, ONION AND BEER MARMALADE

2 teaspoons olive oil
2 onions, chopped
1 teaspoon ground ginger
¼ teaspoon salt
⅛ teaspoon ground red pepper
2 apples, peeled and chopped
1 bottle (12 ounces) craft-brewed lager
2 tablespoons packed brown sugar

1. Heat oil in large skillet over medium-high heat. Add onions; cook and stir 5 minutes or until just beginning to brown. Stir in ginger, salt and ground red pepper.

2. Reduce heat to medium; add apples, lager and brown sugar. Cover; cook 5 minutes. Uncover; cook 10 minutes or until liquid is almost evaporated and apples are tender, stirring occasionally. Serve warm.

WIENER SCHNITZEL
MAKES 4 SERVINGS

½ cup all-purpose flour

½ teaspoon salt

¼ teaspoon black pepper

2 eggs, beaten

¾ cup seasoned dry bread crumbs

4 slices veal scallopini (about 4 ounces each)

2 tablespoons butter

1 tablespoon olive oil

1 cup craft-brewed brown ale

2 tablespoons capers, drained

1 lemon, quartered (optional)

1. Combine flour, salt and pepper in shallow dish; mix well. Place eggs in separate shallow dish and bread crumbs in another shallow dish. Pat veal dry. Dredge each slice in flour mixture, dip in eggs and then coat with bread crumbs.

2. Heat butter and oil in large skillet over medium-high heat. Add veal; cook 3 to 4 minutes or until cooked through, turning once. Remove to plate; keep warm.

3. Add ale to skillet. Bring to a boil over medium-high heat, stirring to scrape up browned bits from bottom of pan. Cook until mixture is slightly thickened. Add capers; remove from heat. Spoon sauce over veal. Garnish with lemon wedges.

BEER-BRAISED OSSO BUCCO

MAKES 4 SERVINGS

½ cup all-purpose flour

1½ teaspoon salt, divided

1 teaspoon black pepper, divided

4 veal shanks (about 3 pounds), cut into 1-inch rounds

3 tablespoons canola oil

3 carrots, chopped

3 stalks celery, chopped

1 large onion, sliced

2 cloves garlic, minced

2 tablespoons tomato paste

1 bottle (12 ounces) craft-brewed amber ale

2 cups beef broth

1 bay leaf

Grated peel of 1 lemon

Mashed potatoes

Chopped fresh parsley

1. Preheat oven to 325°F. Combine flour, 1 teaspoon salt and ½ teaspoon pepper in large bowl. Add veal shanks; turn to coat with flour mixture.

2. Heat oil in large ovenproof saucepan or Dutch oven over medium-high heat. Brown veal shanks in batches 4 to 6 minutes. Remove and set aside. Reduce heat to medium. Add carrots, celery and onion; cook and stir about 5 minutes or until softened. Add garlic; cook and stir 1 minute. Stir in tomato paste. Add beer, scraping up browned bits from bottom of pan. Return shanks to pan.

3. Add broth, bay leaf, lemon peel, remaining ½ teaspoon salt and ½ teaspoon pepper to saucepan. Bring to a boil over high heat. Cover tightly. Bake 2½ to 3 hours or until fork-tender. Remove shanks from saucepan and place in soup bowls. Strain sauce. Return to saucepan; boil until reduced to about 2 cups. Place scoop of mashed potatoes next to shanks. Pour sauce over meat and potatoes. Sprinkle with parsley.

METRIC CONVERSION CHART

VOLUME MEASUREMENTS (dry)

$\frac{1}{8}$ teaspoon = 0.5 mL
$\frac{1}{4}$ teaspoon = 1 mL
$\frac{1}{2}$ teaspoon = 2 mL
$\frac{3}{4}$ teaspoon = 4 mL
1 teaspoon = 5 mL
1 tablespoon = 15 mL
2 tablespoons = 30 mL
$\frac{1}{4}$ cup = 60 mL
$\frac{1}{3}$ cup = 75 mL
$\frac{1}{2}$ cup = 125 mL
$\frac{2}{3}$ cup = 150 mL
$\frac{3}{4}$ cup = 175 mL
1 cup = 250 mL
2 cups = 1 pint = 500 mL
3 cups = 750 mL
4 cups = 1 quart = 1 L

VOLUME MEASUREMENTS (fluid)

1 fluid ounce (2 tablespoons) = 30 mL
4 fluid ounces ($\frac{1}{2}$ cup) = 125 mL
8 fluid ounces (1 cup) = 250 mL
12 fluid ounces (1$\frac{1}{2}$ cups) = 375 mL
16 fluid ounces (2 cups) = 500 mL

WEIGHTS (mass)

$\frac{1}{2}$ ounce = 15 g
1 ounce = 30 g
3 ounces = 90 g
4 ounces = 120 g
8 ounces = 225 g
10 ounces = 285 g
12 ounces = 360 g
16 ounces = 1 pound = 450 g

DIMENSIONS

$\frac{1}{16}$ inch = 2 mm
$\frac{1}{8}$ inch = 3 mm
$\frac{1}{4}$ inch = 6 mm
$\frac{1}{2}$ inch = 1.5 cm
$\frac{3}{4}$ inch = 2 cm
1 inch = 2.5 cm

OVEN TEMPERATURES

250°F = 120°C
275°F = 140°C
300°F = 150°C
325°F = 160°C
350°F = 180°C
375°F = 190°C
400°F = 200°C
425°F = 220°C
450°F = 230°C

BAKING PAN SIZES

Utensil	Size in Inches/Quarts	Metric Volume	Size in Centimeters
Baking or Cake Pan (square or rectangular)	8×8×2	2 L	20×20×5
	9×9×2	2.5 L	23×23×5
	12×8×2	3 L	30×20×5
	13×9×2	3.5 L	33×23×5
Loaf Pan	8×4×3	1.5 L	20×10×7
	9×5×3	2 L	23×13×7
Round Layer Cake Pan	8×1½	1.2 L	20×4
	9×1½	1.5 L	23×4
Pie Plate	8×1¼	750 mL	20×3
	9×1¼	1 L	23×3
Baking Dish or Casserole	1 quart	1 L	—
	1½ quart	1.5 L	—
	2 quart	2 L	—